Black Pow-Wow

FOR YOU
I OFFER
THIS poem
FOR YOU
 ARE IN
 DEED
 IN
 NEED
OF A
  black poem

Black Pow - Wow JAZZ POEMS BY TED JOANS

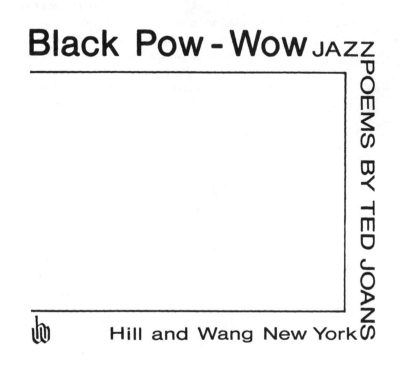

Hill and Wang New York

To
Langston Hughes
and allyall

CONTENTS

Black Pow-Wow

THE TRUTH

IF YOU SHOULD SEE A   M A N

walking down a crowded

street
        talking
                ALOUD

TO HIMSELF

                DON'T RUN
                        IN THE

OPPOSITE DIRECTION

                        BUT RUN

TOWARD HIM

            for he is a

                POET

You have NOTHING to
                FEAR

FROM THE

            P O E T
                BUT THE

            T R U T H

PASSED ON BLUES: HOMAGE TO A POET

the sound of black music
the sad soft low moan of jazz ROUND BOUT MIDNIGHT
the glad heavy fat screaming song of happy blues
That was the world of Langston Hughes

the mood indigo candle flame
the rough racy hot gut bucket riff tune AFTER HOURS
the fast swinging rapid rocking riff rumping blues
That was the world of Langston Hughes

the funky butt grind
the every night jitterbug jiving gliding his Trouble In Mind
the brown black beige high yaller bouncer's shoes
That was the world of Langston Hughes

the sonata of Harlem
the concerto to shoulder bones/pinto beans/ hamhocks In the Dark
the slow good bouncing grooves
That was the world of Langston Hughes

the elephant laugh
the rain forest giggles under a switchblade downpour
the zoot suited conked head razor throat Stompin' at the Savoy
the colored newspaper with no good news
That was the world of Langston Hughes

the Jess B. Semple hip sneer
the bassist/drummer/pianist/guitarist/rhythm on top of Caldonia
the take it, shake it, rattle, lay back & make it (or lose!)
That was the world of Langston Hughes

the big black mouth
the pawnshop/butcher shop/likker shop/ . . . Bebop!
the rats in the rice, roaches of reefers on relief amused
That was the world of Langston Hughes

the Manhattan subway stool
the naked thigh, double breasted one button Roll On To Jesus!
the poolroom chalk & click, fat chick wobble in cigarette tar baby
                                                                                crews
That was the world of Langston Hughes

the chain gang jingle
the evil laughter against the atomic Honeydripper
the brownstone tenement cold filthy frozen winter hell ghetto dues   3
That was the world of Langston Hughes

the uh-huh, Oo-wee, oh yeah of hot climax
the hustlers haunt, prostitutes pimp, bitter Sweet Georgia Brown
the hep hip hi junkie tongue tied black eyed bruise
That was the world of Langston Hughes

the sounds of dangerous black humor
the swift sharp flash of Afroamerica Struttin' Wid Sum Bar-B-Q
the Presence Africaine, Harlem Jew, chittlin switching cruise
That was the world of Langston Hughes

the fried fish'n'chicken boogie woogie
the store front church Cadillac/wig wearing/ gospel truths/When
                                                They Crucified My Lord
the nigger loving Thirties, dozens by the dirties on ofay's muse
That was the world of Langston Hughes

the rent party good-timing crowd
the shout strut twist turning loud raving but Ain't Misbehavin'
the darkie, jig; coon, hidden shadowy spade drowned in booze
That was the world of Langston Hughes

the taker of A Trains
the sticker upper, alley cat, hustler, poolshark cleanhead Hucklebuck
the cornbread smell, grits, greens, watermelon,
                                                spare ribs never refused!
That was the world of Langston Hughes

the cool crowded summer solo horn
the red rattled raisin around the sun/migrated Dixieland
Strange Fruit
the jim crow/black crow/Ol' Crow/ moonshine splo/niggers
cant go or choose
That was the world of Langston Hughes

the sweaty hard-working muscle making black back breaking hard
labour hump
the bold bright colors on ebony nappy head big titty itty
bitty Liza Jane
the millions and millions raising up strong been done wrong
too long pointing
the abused body at slum lord! war lord! police lord! Oh Lord, all
guilty and accused!
THAT WAS THE WORLD OF THE POET LANGSTON HUGHES
BLACK DUES! BLACK BLUES! BLACK NEWS!
THAT WAS THE WORLD OF THE GREATEST BLACK POET
LANGSTON HUGHES

4

O GREAT BLACK MASQUE

O great black masque   that is me
that travels with me in spirit
your big eyes that see tomorrows
saw yesterdays   and gazes at now
O great black masque of my soul
those ears have heard the clink
of slaves chains   and the moans
of sorrow   of our past   but those
same ears   can hear our now
O great black masque   that is   me
you who copulated with Europe's science
and now dynamically demysterfies Europe
O great black masque   who is our
ancestors   with your cave mouth
filled with sharp teeth   to chew
the ropes that bind our hands and minds
O great black masque   you that grins
you that always wins   the thrower of
seven cowries   and two black eyed dice
O great black masque   who says that it
half past pink since white is not a color
O great black masque   that carried me from Bouake
to Alabama and back   From Mali to Manhattan
O great black masque that dances in me day and night
O black masque of urban guerillas and forest gorillas
O black masque that screams in joy at childbirth and
opens up to the rays of the sun   O great black masque
your sharp blade tongue burns war makers buildings
You who stand guard to African breast and soul
O great black masque give us our blacker heavens/
release our minds from borrowed white hells/ O great
black masque of Africa   O great black masque of all
black people   O beautiful black masque Our own black
truth

HOW DO YOU WANT YOURS?

DEAR MR & MRS UNITED STATES   or   GREETINGS TO YOU ALL
    OF AMERICA
YOU IN YOUR COMFORTABLE ALL WHITE or ALL AMERICAN
    NEIGHBORHOOD,suburb,township
HAVE YOU FINISHED HAVING YOUR BALL AT THIRD WORLD'S
    EXPENSE?
HAVE YOU TAKEN EVERYTHING FOR WHAT IT WAS WORTH
    INCLUDING THIS RETRIBUTION?
[SOFT FLOWERS THAT SMELL DURING THE NIGHT   MOUNTED ON
    STEEL FRAMES
WITH R.I.P. AND YOUR NAME   AWAIT YOU FLANKED BY GALLONS
    OF GUILT TEARS AND SAD SNOT]
DEAR MR & MRS AMERICA OF YESTERDAY AND TODAY FOR THERE
    IS NO MORE GUARANTEE OF YOUR
TOMORROW   THATS WHY YOU AND INSECTS 'LONG FOR
    YESTERDAY' WHEN,FOR YOU CRIME DID PAY
ARE YOU READY TO GO ? ARE YOU SICK AND TIRED OF IT ALL ?
    YOUR GAME IS OVER, YOU LOST!
I GREET YOU WITH A QUICK DEATH IN YOUR HOME OF THE
    DEPRAVED LAND OF THE WHITE FREE
THE THIRD WORLD HAS LET YOU SHOW YOUR BLOODSTAINED
    HANDS   PHYSICAL,MENTALLY GUILTY
[SOFT FLOWERS THAT SMELL DURING THE NIGHT   MOUNTED ON
    STEEL FRAMES WITH R.I.P.
AND YOUR NAME   AWAIT   YOU   FLANKED BY GALLONS OF
    GUILT TEARS AND SAD SNOT]
YOUR TIME IS UP . . . THE KNOCK ON YOUR DOOR IS . . . DEATH
    DEATH COMES TO YOU AMERICA
MR & MRS AMERICA WHO ACTIVELY SUPPORTED THE US REPUBLIC
    AND FOR WHAT IT STANDS
YOU THE WHITE   OR NEGRO INDIVIDUAL BELIEVER IN THE
    AMERICAN NATION IMPERIALIST HANDS
DEATH IS HERE BEFORE YOU/DEATH IS WHAT YOU NEED   WHAT
    YOULL GET/WHAT YOU WERE DESTINED FOR/
DEATH DEATH DEATH/DEATH FOR YOU MR & MRS AMERICA
    DEATH HAS FOUND YOU OUT THROUGH YOU
[SOFT FLOWERS THAT SMELL DURING THE NIGHT MOUNTED ON A
    STEEL FRAME WITH R.I.P. AND

YOUR NAME   AWAIT YOU   FLANKED BY GALLONS OF GUILT TEARS
    AND SAD SNOT]
YOU ARE ALL GOING TO DIE   WHY CRY   YOU ARE ALL GOING TO
    DIE   DEATH IS READY FOR YOU
DEATH HAS ALWAYS HAD YOU AT THE TOP OF THE DEATH LIST
    YOU WILL SOON BE NO MORE
THERES NO REASON TO STAND THERE SMOKING   DEATH AINT
    JOKING YOU ARE GOING TO DIE DIE
[SOFT FLOWERS THAT SMELL DURING THE NIGHT MOUNTED ON
    STEEL FRAMES   WITH R.I.P.

AND YOUR NAME AWAIT YOU   FLANKED BY GALLONS OF GUILT
    TEARS AND SAD SNOT]
DEATH CAN NOT BE PREVENTED   YOU ARE GOING TO DIE WHITE
    GIRL   YOU ARE GOING TO DIE
WHITE BOY   YOU ARE GOING TO DIE WHITE MAN   YOU ARE GOING
    TO DIE WHITE WOMAN YOU ARE
ALL GOING TO DIE   NEGRO WOMAN TRYING TO LOOK,TALK, AND
    ACT WHITE YOU ARE GOING TO
DIE   NEGRO MAN   WITH YOUR INDIVIDUAL NIGGER MONEY
    GITTING PLAN YOU ARE GOING TO DIE
DEATH IS HERE AS YOU LISTEN TO THIS POEM DEATH IS EACH
    WORD YOU HEAR DEATH SINKS INTO
EARS, YOUR EYES, YOUR ASSHOLE IS FULLA DEATH YOUR SHIT
    SMELLS OF DEATH, SNIFF IT!
DEATH IS INSIDE YOUR DOOMED BODY   YOUR DOOMED WHITE
    SOUL   YOUR TEETH HAVE DEATH
BETWEEN THEM SAME AS YOUR TOES   YOUR BONES,PORES,
    BREATH, AND EVEN YOUR SPERM IS
FULLA DEATH DEATH   DEATH INVENTED CIGARETTES TO HURRY
    YOUR DEATH
DEATH CREATED CAPITALISM AND WHITE COMMUNISM TO SPREAD
    DEATH
DEATH MADE YOUR SKIN COLORLESS TO RESEMBLE DEATH
NEGROES THAT LEAN WHITE,LOVE WHITE, WILL HAVE WHITE
    NIGHTS OF DEATH
DEATH DARES YOU TO DROP DEAD BEFORE DEATH
DEATH IS NOT WAITING FOR YOU IN THE DARK BUT IN YOUR
    WHITE LIGHT OF DEATH
YOU ARE ALL GOING TO DIE   YOU ALL GONNA DIE DAMN YOU
    DIE   WHY TRY TO ESCAPE DEATH??
[SOFT FLOWERS THAT SMELL DURING THE NIGHT   MOUNTED ON
    STEEL FRAMES   WITH R.I.P.

AND YOUR NAME   AWAIT   YOU   FLANKED BY GALLONS OF GUILT
    TEARS   AND   SAD SNOT]
DEATH IS GETTING HOLD OF YOUR EMOTIONS/RIGHT NOW/WHILE
    YOU LISTEN TO DEATH
DEATH SMILES AT THE GUILTY CAUSE YOU ARE CHILDREN OF
    DEATH   DEATH IS YOUR NATIONAL
WHITE DADDY HE IS FILLED UP WITH DEATH/DEATH IS THE MAN
    BEHIND THE COUNTER/WHITE AND
GUILTY OF ROBBERY,EXPLOITATION, AND MURDER/DEATH WILL
    GET HIM   DEATH IS AFTER YOU TOO
DEATH IS WITH YOU IN THE MORNING   DEATH IS WITH YOU AT THE
    TABLE   DEATH IS NEVER ALONE
DEATH IS CROWDING IN ON YOU   YOU CAN SNEER AT DEATH
    DEATH DIGS YOUR SNEERS
YOU CAN LAUGH AT DEATH/ THAT JUST MAKES DEATH'S JOB
    EASIER   DEATH IS NO LONGER
COMING DEATH IS ALREADY HERE   DEATH IS WITH YOU THE
    GUILTY   THE POET IS THE JUDGE
HEAR THE POETS WORDS   DO THEY SING OR DO THEY STING??
    DEATH IS/IS AND WILL ALWAYS
BE STRICTLY FOR YOU   YOU BROUGHT DEATH TO THE EARTH
    WITH YOUR VICIOUSNESS   YOU
WHO LOVED WAR YOU WHO DESTROYED COLORED PEOPLE   AND
    YOU WHO CONTINUE TO DO SO
DEATH IS YOURS/DEATH IS YOUR TRADITION/DEATH IS THE
    ONLY THING THAT YOU WILL GIVE
AWAY FREELY/DEATH IS ALL YOU NEED   THIS IS YOUR TIME TO
    DIE/DEATH DEATH DEATH
[SOFT FLOWERS THAT SMELL DURING THE NIGHT MOUNTED ON
    STEEL FRAMES   WITH R.I.P.
AND YOUR NAME   AWAIT YOU FLANKED   BY GALLONS OF GUILT
    TEARS AND SAD SNOT]
YOU OF THE WHITE WILL DIE THIS VERY NIGHT/DEATH HAS
    CHOSEN YOU/SO DIE,DIE,DIE,DIE!

8

THE .38

i hear the man downstairs slapping the hell out of his stupid

wife again

i hear him push   and shove her around the overcrowded room
i hear her scream and beg for mercy
i hear him tell her *there is no mercy*
i hear the blows as they land on her beautiful body
i hear her screams and pleas
i hear glasses and pots and pans falling
i hear her fleeing from the room
i hear them running up the stairs
i hear her outside MY DOOR!
i hear him coming toward her outside MY DOOR!!
i hear her banging on MY DOOR!!!
i hear him bang her head on MY DOOR!
I HEAR HIM TRYING TO DRAG HER AWAY FROM MY DOOR
i hear her hands desperate on my door knob
i hear him bang her head against my door
i hear him drag her away from my door
i hear him drag her down the stairs
i hear her head bounce from step to step
i hear him drag that beautiful body
i hear them again in their room
THEN   i hear a loud slap   across her face (i guess)
i hear her groan . . . . then
i hear the eerie silence
i hear   him open   the top drawer   of his bureau   the .38 lives

there!!!

i hear the fast beat of my heart
i hear the drops of perspiration fall from my brow
i hear him yell: I WARNED YOU!!!
i hear him pull her limp body across their overcrowded room

i hear the springs of their bed creak from the weight of her beautiful
body
i hear him say DAMN YOU, I WARNED YOU, AND NOW IT'S TOO
LATE
THEN   I HEAR   THE   LOUD REPORT OF THE THIRTY EIGHT
CALIBER REVOLVER!!!
i hear it again and again the Smith & Wessen
i hear the BANG BANG BANG BANG   of four death-dealing
bullets!
i hear my heart beat faster and louder . . . . and   then again
i hear the eerie silence
i hear him walk out of their overcrowded room
i hear him walk up the steps
i hear him come toward M Y D O O R !
i hear   his hand on my door knob
i hear my door knob click
i hear the door slowly open
i hear   him step into my room
i hear him standing there/ breathing heavy/ and taking aim
I HEAR THE CLICK OF THE THIRTY EIGHT JUST BEFORE
THE FIRING PIN HITS THE DEATH-DEALING BULLET!!
I HEAR THE LOUD BLAST OF THE POWDER EXPLODING IN
THE CHAMBER OF THE .38!
I HEAR THE HEAVY LEAD NOSE OF THE BULLET SWIFTLY
CUTTING ITS WAY THROUGH THE BARREL OF THE .38!
I HEAR IT EMERGE OUT INTO SPACE FROM THE .38!
I HEAR THE BULLET OF DEATH FLYING TOWARD MY HEAD
THE .38!!
I HEAR IT COMING FASTER THAN SOUND THE .38!

I HEAR IT COMING CLOSER TO MY SWEATY FOREHEAD
THE .38!
I HEAR AND NOW I CAN SEE IT THE .38!

10

I HEAR ITS WEIRD WHISTLE THE .38!

I HEAR IT JUST ONE INCH FROM MY HEAD THE .38!!

I HEAR IT   GIVE OFF   A   LITTLE STEAMLIKE   NOISE
        WHEN IT CUTS THROUGH MY   SWEAT   THE .38!!!

I HEAR IT SINGE MY SKIN AS IT ENTERS MY HEAD
                                    THE .38!!!!

11

... AND   I HEAR DEATH SAYING   HELLO, I'M   *HERE!*

LETS GET VIOLENT!

LETS GET VIOLENT!   AND ATTACK THE   WHITEWASH
    !CING CAKED

ON OUR BLACK MINDS

12   LETS GET SO VIOLENT   THAT WE LEAVE that white way
    of thinking

IN   THE TOILET BENEATH OUR BLACK BEHINDS   LETS
    GET VIOLENT!

FOR THE VIET CONGO

THEY CAME OUT OF NEANDERTHALIC CAVES
DRAGGING THEIR WOMEN BY THE HAIR
THEY HAD JUST FEASTED ON FLESH
OF A CHILD(Dr.Spock did not mention
the recipe in his CHILDCARE BK.)

THEY CAME OUT INSANELY COURAGEOUS
WELL ARMED THUS BRAVE/MINDS CROWDED
WITH THIRST FOR BLOOD ADVENTURE
LUST   AND BELIEFS IN WHITE GOD

THEY   NOW CLAD IN CHRISTIAN WAR COATS
FLYING PIECES OF CLOTH CALLING IT FLAG
KNEELING/SALUTING/ AND RESPECTING   IT
AS THOUGH IT WAS A WOMAN OR TREE . . . . . THEY CAME/TO OUR
    SHORES/ AND THE THIRD WORLD KNOWS WHO THAT "THEY"
                                                          WAS

THEY CAME TO STEAL/and they stole
TO KILL/AND THEY KILLED/TO PLANT
LIES/and they did/RAPING NOT ONLY
THIRD WORLD WOMEN AND CHILDREN BUT
OUR SHEEP COULD GET NO SLEEP WHEN
THEY CAME . . . . AND THE THIRD WORLD KNOWS   WHO THAT
                                                "THEY" WAS

THEY CAME TOOK THE LAND /AND SET ASIDE
THE BEST FOR THEMSELVES/THEIR LIVING
IMAGES HAVE MAINTAINED THEIR STATUS QUO
TODAY/WITH GUN THEY ENSLAVED US OR
CREATED THIRD RATE IMITATIONS OF THEMSELVES
INTEGRATION OF THE IMAGINATION/MELTING POT
TAKING EVERYTHING WE HAD AND GOT/THIEVES
THEY ARE . . . . they came   Yes and the THIRD WORLD knows who
                                                that "THEY" is

THEY CAME WITH SYPHILIS ON THE
END OF THEIR BLONDE TONGUES AND
OPEN SORES OF GONORRHEA SPEWING
PUS FROM THEIR SKY BLUE EYES/IT
WAS HIGHLY ADVERTISED /SOUGHT AFTER
IN SUPERMARKETS/COMMUNISTS MEETINGS/

HOLLYWOOD FILMS AND RADIO BLARED
THAT IT WAS BEST FOR ALL/BECAUSE THEY
CAME WITH IT . . . . . THEY CAME   YES,AND THE THIRD WORLD
                                   KNOWS WHO THEY ARE
THEY HAD RACISM IN ALL FORMS,THEY
FORCED THEIR LAW & ORDER THROUGH
PROCLAMATIONS,CONSTITUTIONS,AND
BIASED CHARTERS . . THEIR LANGUAGES
WERE THE ONLY LANGUAGES USED THUS
THEY ABUSED,MISUSED, AND JAILED
THOSE OF US WHO REBELLED   OR REFUSED
YES THEY CAME AND THE THIRD WORLD KNOWS EXACTLY WHO
                                          THEY ARE
TODAY THEY HAVE CREATED A PILL/A BOMB/AND AN EVIL SLOGAN
POPULATION EXPLOSION/THEIR GOAL IS TO DESTROY MANKIND/
                                          THEY
HAVE NO REASON TO LIVE/THEY ARE BORED WITH LIFE/THEY
                                          CAN NOT
LOVE/THEY CAN NOT FACE THE WORLD WITHOUT BEING DRUGGED
                                          OR
DRUNK/WEAPONS TO DESTROY IS ALL THEY'VE GOT/AND YET THE
                                          THIRD WORLD
FEARS THEM NOT/THE THIRD WORLD EVERY NON-WHITE MAN/
                                    WOMAN/BOY & GIRL
THE MAJORITY OF HUMAN BEINGS ON THIS OUR EARTH/WE STAND
                                          READY TO DO
WHAT HAS TO BE DONE/WE SHALL NOT STOP OUR REVOLUTION/
                                    UNTIL WE HAVE WON
WE OF THE THIRD WORLD/KNOW WHO THEY ARE/WHO WORKS WITH
                              THEM/AND   WHAT SHALL BE DONE

14

THE P I T OF COLD BROTHER BULLSHIT

They call themselves   Black Upper Class
They walk/talk/ and act as though
they never nose blow/sweat/   or
release belly(I meant stomach)   gas
They of Wash.D.C. nigger high ass
They think they've made it
up white imitation ladder at last
Those cold brothers down in D.C.
We gotta pull their coatails/and FAST!

15

LUMUMBA LIVES   L U M U M B A   L I V E S !!

FOR HE   LUMUMBA   PERHAPS   LUMUMBA   LIKE THEIR
johnbrown made hasty hurry ups

FOR his   LUMUMBA   PEOPLE OF   LUMUMBA   BLACK
AFRICA   WOKE UP ABRUPTLY

16 SO HE LUMUMBA   ON PERHAPS ABE LINCOLN'S BIRTHDAY
LUMUMBA WAS MADE   A   MARTYR

AND
NOW   LUMUMBA SHALL LIVE   FOREVER
in the BLACK   in the white   in the YELLOW   and in the RED
for these
PEOPLE   KNOW that patrice L U M U M B A   IS   NOT   DEAD!
LUMUMBA LIVES LUMUMBA LIVES LUMUMBA LIVES
LUMUMBA LIVES LUMUMBA LIVES!!

UH HUH

THERE IT IS
UH HUH
YEP
THAT'S IT
UH HUH
THERE IS NO DOUBT ABOUT IT
UH HUH
THAT'S IT!!
UH HUH!
YES SIREE
UH HUH
MAN, THIS IS IT!
UH HUH
THE REAL THING
UH HUH
NO SHIT
HERE
UH HUH
THE REAL BIT!!
UH HUH
HERE IT IS
UH HUH
A FACT
UH HUH
RIGHT BEFORE THE EYES
UH HUH
THIS IS REALLY IT
UH HUH
YEP YEP
A TRUTH
UH HUH
REALITY!
UH HUH
WELL I'LL BE DAMNED
UH HUH
HERE NOW
UH HUH THIS UH HUH NOW UH HUH THERE UH HUH
    UH HUH UH HUH UH HUH!!
THE   COLORED   WAITING   ROOM!!!!!

THE ATHLETE

to Harry Edwards

HE RAN FASTER   HE JUMPED HIGHER   HE THREW
   FARTHER   HE FOUGHT HARDER
HE ENDURED LONGER

                        AND YET   THEY TRIED TO
   KEEP THIS HUMAN   BACK
NOT BECAUSE OF SOMETHING

                             UNJUST HE'D DONE   BUT
   BECAUSE HE WAS BLACK
WHEN HE COULD LIVE NO LONGER

                         THEY IMMEDIATELY
   TRANSPLANTED HIS HEART
IT WAS STRONGER!

              [EVEN IN DEATH THEY WORKED HIM]
     transplant proved
Whites to be weaker

               THUS *CAN NOT LIVE* MUCH LONGER!

18

NEW NAMES

THESE STREETS/ THESE WIDE BOULEVARDS/ AND LONG
  AVENUES:
  DUBOIS . . . . ROBESON . . . . GARVEY . . . .
               MALCOLM X
  MARTIN LUTHER KING . . . . JOE LOUIS . . . .
              JACK JOHNSON
THATS WHAT THEIR NAMES SHOULD BE
THESE STREETS/ THESE WIDE BOULEVARDS/ AND LONG
  AVENUES

THESE PARKS/ THESE INTERSECTIONS/ AND REST STOPS:
  JAMES P. JOHNSON . . . . LESTER YOUNG . . . .
             BUD POWELL
DINAH WASHINGTON . . . . CHARLIE CHRISTIAN . . . .
           CHARLIE PARKER
THATS WHAT THEIR NAMES SHOULD BE

NOT WHITE NAMES OR NUMBERS   LETS MAKE HARLEM'S
  STREET NAMES F R E E

TWO WORDS

some of THEM fear   Black poetswords   now that Blackpoets dont
                                    write in code or metaphor
Blackpoets who imitated   whitepoets from SHAKESPEARE   to
                                    DYLAN THOMAS
thus deny their own Blackfolklore
now the   whites   have reason to get   UPTIGHT   and   some of
                                    THEM   COWER
when   a   BLACKPOET   screams   or whispers   those TWO
                                    beautiful words BLACKPOWER!!

NO MAD TALK

AT TIMES   ME   FEEL   LIKE ME   JES BACK FROM
                                    ANOTHER MOTHER PLANET
CAUSE WHEN   ME   TALK/   ABOUT ME WALK/ IN
                                    MOTHERLAND A F R I C A
from TANGIERS TO ALGIERS/   from OUAGADOUGOU TO
                                    TIMBUCTOO/from
ABIDJAN TO KAIROUAN/ from TRIPOLI TO WADIDI/ or to
                                    a place called TIT!
dey look at me real dumb ME WANTA   SHOUT   "AW   SHIT!"
                                    YET INSTEAD
I PLEAD HOPING THAT MY BROTHERS AND SISTERS
                                    ABOUT A F R I C A DO
PLEASE READ! CAUSE ME NOT A MAN   FROM OUTER
                                    SPACE ME JES BEEN TRAVELING
AMONGST OUR BEAUTIFUL BLACK RACE   from TANGIERS
                                    to ALGIERS/OUAGADOUGOU to
TIMBUCTOO/ABIDJAN to KAIROUAN/ ACCRA to DAKAR/
                                    CONAKRY to MOPTI/BAMAKO to
KANO/ TIZNIT to TESSALIT/ MEKNES to AGADES/ FORT
                                    LAMY to BENGHAZI/ CAIRO to
BOBO-DIOLASSO/ and from a place   called T I T

IT AM THAT WAY

I SWEAR TO GOD BABY   THAT IT REALLY MAKES
    ME MAD WHEN SOMETIMES
IT BE THAT WAY   FOR EXAMPLE/   as a sample/ to
    make a description—ample
I swear to god   it really be like that, like what, you may
    ask, for an
example/ as a sample/ to make a description——ample:
WHEN IT BE YOU EXPECT OF ME TO TAKE YOU OUT TO
    DINNER
AND YOU CHOOSE THE MOST EXPENSIVE DISHES ON THE
    MENU (THATS WHAT YOU DO DO!)
OR WHEN YOU ORDER THAT DRINK THAT CAUSES THE
    BARTENDER TO SEARCH AND CONCOCT,
SHAKE AND MAKE . . . MONEY FOR ALCOHOL/ YOU AND
    YOUR DAMN MIXED DRINKS
IF YOU ARE A BLACK REVOLUTION WHY DO YOU NEED
    ANYTHING "MIXED" ANYWAY YOU MUST BE
MIXED UP DONT YOU KNOW THAT MIXED THIS AND THAT
    DONT WORK LIKE MARRIAGES ANYWAY
BUT I KNOW IT JES BE THAT WAY SOMETIMES/YOU KNOW
    HOW IT IS/NOW,DONTCHA?
THE WAY YOU FEEL ABOUT WHITE WOMEN'S CLOTHES
    LED BY WHITE FASHION BY YOUR BLACK NOSE
SOMETIMES YOU GOT YOUR HAIR ALL NATURAL AND NICE
    BUT YOUR DRESS SO SHORT
I THOUGHT IT WAS YOUR BLOUSE OR YOUR SHOES HEELS
    SO HIGH THAT I HAVE TO
SMOKE POT TO GET UP THERE IN THE AIR WHERE YOU AT
    YEAH I KNOW IT BE THAT WAY
SOMETIMES   AND SOMETIMES IT BE LIKE THIS: YOU
    GREET ME WITHOUT A KISS

OR WHEN YOU DO ME BAD THUS MAKING ME MAD   WHEN
    YOU DONT WANT TO WALK ALIDDLE BIT FAR
YOU EVEN REFUSE THE SUBWAY TELLING ME TO CALL A

TAXI   PUTTING ME DOWN WITH A LOWRATE
FROWN FOR NOT   GOING IN DEBT BUYING A GODAMN
    C A R   YEAH BABY IT SHOW BE THAT WAY
SOMETIMES   SO DONT CALL ME CHEAP WHEN I REFUSE
    TO SPEND MONEY THAT I AINT GOT
DONT NAG RIP AND RAP OR ACT LIKE A BITCH   AND MAKE
    ME HOT   DONT EXPLOIT YOUR
POOR BLACK REVOLUTIONARY MAN   OR GIT MAD AND
    TURN COLD   JUST REMEMBER THAT AFTER
THE REVOLUTION WE'LL HAVE SOMETHING MORE
    VALUABLE THAN GOLD . . . . F R E E D O M !
yet i know sister soul . . . you show be that bitchy way some-most-
    many of the TIMES, YEAH!-

EUROPE ON FIVE DOLLARS A DAY

to Arthur Frommer

YOU VISIT EUROPE ON FIVE DOLLARS A DAY?
YOU *CAN* VISIT EUROPE ON   FIVE DOLLARS   A DAY
YOU CAN VISIT EUROPE ON FIVE DOLLARS A DAY?
YOU   *CAN*   VISIT EUROPE ON FIVE DOLLARS A   DAY
CAN YOU VISIT EUROPE ON FIVE DOLLAR   DAY?
YOU CAN VISIT EUROPE ON FIVE DOLLAR DAY   23
CAN YOU FIVE DOLLAR EUROPE ON VISIT
YOU CAN VISIT FIVE DOLLAR DAY
CAN YOU DOLLAR EUROPE ON FIVE?
DAY DOLLARS FIVE ON EUROPE
CAN YOU VISIT FIVE DOLLARS?
YOU CAN VISIT FIVE DOLLARS
FIVE DOLLARS A VISIT
FIVE DOLLARS A VISIT FIVE DOLLARS A VISIT
CAN YOU DOLLAR VISIT
EUROPE DAY
VISIT DAY
CAN DAY   CAN YOU DOLLAR   CAN YOU VISIT
DOLLAR CAN   DOLLAR CAN DOLLAR DOLLAR CAN
                    DOLLAR CAN DOLLAR CAN DOLLAR CAN
CAN YOU DOLLAR CAN YOU DOLLAR CAN YOU DOLLAR
                    CAN YOU DOLLAR CAN YOU DOLLAR?
YOU CAN YOU CAN YOU CAN YOU CAN YOU CAN YOU CAN
                    YOU CAN YOU CAN YOU CAN
DO   C U M !

WHITEYES ON BLACKTHIGHS

I KNOW YOU DIG DARK ME
I KNOW YOU WANT A TASTE
BUT IF YOU LAY A HAND
ON   ME
I'LL RUN
A RAZOR BLADE
SEVEN TIMES
A CROSS
YOUR PALE
CRACKER
FACE

24

THE UBIQUITOUS LIONS

to O. Egbuna

There are four lions   at Trafalgar Square   stolen symbols
    that do not
bare any-kinda resemblance   to European royalty
These four lions   at Trafalgar Square   with whom European
    queens and
kings   try to identify   are African   and very very B L A C K
The four lions at Trafalgar Square   sit regally/lazy/
    and cooly   gaze
whilst mini-skirted tourists slide between their wide spread paws
although they have a hip sneer   across their majestic black jaws
These four lions at Trafalgar Square   bigger than young elephants
heavier than fourteen Rolls Royces   have nothing a-tall to do with
chalk-white kings or Europeans horses   an auto roar imitates their
    black voices
These four black lions   of Africa   now sitting in London
    dreary town
lookout in four directions   at international tourists
    pose near   or
around   for the photo shot   these lions DO NOT FROWN!
The four black lions   at Trafalgar Square   have heard and seen
white demonstrations/meeting & rally lost and won
they've witnessed white man's pro & con   white guilt & fears
Nearby stands the South African Building and closer still is
    a Hippy church
For U.S.A. Civil Rites   and Biafra white nigger crocodile shed tears
There are four lions   at Trafalgar Square   they are black   and
    like lions everywhere
on European buildings   pedestals and government seals
These black lions must be free   to attack imperialism and destroy
    that evil deal
Sic'em sic'em lions   git them   white devils who dared to identify
    with thy!

NO MO' KNEEGROW
(Composed while flying over Birmingham; can be sung to the tune of "Oh! Susannah")

I'M   FLYING OVER   ALABAMA   WITH   BLACK POWER IN MY
    LAP

I'M FLYING OVER   ALABAMA   PREPARING THE   GREAT
    BLACK SLAP

ALL   YOU   HONEST   RACISTS   GIT THE HELL OFF MY BACK

'CAUSE I'M   FLYING   OVER   ALABAMA

'CAUSE I'M TIRED   OF   TAKING   CRAP

LA GRANDE GRANNY

she fled   to France and   bared her black soul
international fame was her royal role
Europe recognized her/ made images of her/ adored her/gave her
            medals/and even married her   but none gave her gold
she adopted children   of many cultures and into a big chateau   and
                              bigger debt she went
Europe recognized her/ made images of her/ adored her/ gave her
      medals/married her/and even named perfumes after her   but
                              not one gave her a   cent
she is now old/from struggling   but still beautiful and black
when we get black power   lets bring our Granny Jo back

COLD

ITS COLD   CONCRETELY COLD

IN STONE COLD KILLER COLD NYC

AND ME   CAUGHT COLD HAND   IN AMERICA

CAUGHT BETWEEN   COLD RAIN   COLD WIND   AND   OLD

COLD FRIENDS   WHO DIG   THEIR AMERICAN

COLD PSYCHIC PAIN   ITS   SO DAMN   COLD   DAMP DIRTY

COLD   TURNS ME OLD   CUTS MY BLACK BEAUTY AND SOUL

CAUGHT UP   IN   THE   FOLD OF   COLD   AMERICA

THEY'LL PUT YOU UP —— —— ——T I G H T

to rest your body
  to lay it down
  in   a   bed
  on   a   couch
  or   on   a   floor
  is   very   very
  difficult   to   do
  for   free
  even   with   friends
  like   rhyming
  the   word
  A M E R I C A

GUTTER GAL

HER TEETH   WORE YELLOW SOCKS WITH GREEN TOPS   HER
   RAGGIDY ARMPITS SMELLED OF
PIGFEET   HER   DOUBLE   BREASTED BRA   HAD A   SAFE-T-PIN   IN
   THE BACK

HER STOCKINGS HAD SPLATTERED ABSTRACT PISS STAINS ON
   THEM   HER   METALLIC SKIRT
HURT HER FAT WAIST   HER TURNED OVER SHOES WERE TOO
   TIGHT ON HER TOES   SHE CRIED
SPARKS WHEN SHE RAN   HER HAIR WAS FRIED AS THOUGH IN A PAN
   AND VERY VERY GREASY

HER VOICE WAS WINE-O HOARSE AND T.B. WHEEZY   SHE HAD SPENT
   MOST   HER   THIRTY YEARS
IN WINTER JAILS AND SUMMER GUTTERS   WHEN SHE WAS SOBER
   AND NOT ASHAMED   SHE'D
TELL YOU HER NAME AS SHE STUTTERED   HER EYES WET,PLAID
   RED, AND WRONG   HER EVERY

GESTURE WAS AN ALCOHOLIC DANCE OR SAD SONG   SHE HAD
   NEVER KNOWN WEALTH AND BETTER
HEALTH   UNTIL A HIP BLACK STUDENT TURNED HER AWAY FROM
   DEATH   AND HE TAUGHT HER
TO   BE BEAUTIFUL BY HELPING HERSELF

THEY FORGET TO FAST

THE STATUE OF CHARLIE PARKER   TEN FEET TALL THrEE TONS
                    OF CONCRETE/BRONZE/
AND MARBLE BASE/   STANDS AT   SHERIDAN SQUARE
                           FACING ME
FROM WHERE I SIT   HERE IN TIMBUCTOO   STONED AS THE
                           STATUE!
THE STATUE OF CHARLIE PARKER   WITH ALTO SAX   ACROSS THE
                     CHEST   MAKES ME
RECALL   NUMBER FOUR   BARROW STREET   (REPLACED NOW
                  BY PARKER TOWERS,PITY!)
FOR IT WAS THERE   WHERE WE SHARED: POT/ PAINT/POEMS/MUSIC/
                  FOOD & PLENTY PUSSY
FROM OVER-ANXIOUS OFAY BITCHES
NOW   LATE   EVENING WHITE BIRDS   EAT CRUMBS   SPRINKLED
                    AT THE FEET
OF THE STATUE OF   CHARLIE PARKER   AND THESE LATE EVENING
                  WHITE 'BIRDS' EAT
AND THEY COPY AND THEY CHEAT AND THEY EAT AND THEY COPY
                AND THEY CHEAT AND THEY EAT
AND FINALLY   WITH OVER STUFFED   GUTS   THEY FLY JUST
                  HIGH ENOUGH TO
ALIGHT ON THE   STATUE OF   CHARLIE PARKER   AND THEY SIT
                  AND THEY SHIT!
THEY   FORGET   TOO   FAST

AINT GOT

SHE AINT GOT NO
SHE AINT GOT NO MAN
SHE AINT GOT NO MONEY
SHE AINT GOT NO SCHOOLING
SHE AINT GOT NO RELATIVES
SHE AINT GOT NO RELIGION
SHE AINT GOT HALF AS MUCH AS YOU
SHE AINT OR GONNA GIT NO SCHOOLING
SHE GOT A WHOLE LOT . . . . . . A HALF DOZEN BLACK KIDS . . . SHE
                                                AINT FOOLING
SHE AINT GOT NO FRIENDS
SHE AINT GOT NO ENEMIES
SHE AINT GOT NO JOB
  SHE AINT GOT NOTHING THATS CONFUSING
SHE GOT A HALF A DOZEN BLACK KIDS . . . AND I AINT FOOLING
SHE AINT GOT NO ADDRESS
SHE AINT GOT NO CREDIT
SHE AINT GOT NO WELFARE CHECK
    SHE AINT NEVER DROOLING
    SHE'S GOT HALF DOZEN BLACK KIDS   AND I AINT FOOLING
    SHE AINT GOT NO CAR
    SHE AINT GOT NO MARRIED NAME
    SHE AINT GOT NO UPPITY HANG-UPS
    SHE AINT GOT NO SHAME
    SHE AINT GOT NO PULL
    SHE AINT GOT NO BREAD
    SHE'S GOT A HALF DOZEN BRAVE BLACK CHILDREN
                                THAT HAVE TO BE FED
    YALL BETTER SHARE WHAT YOU GOT WITH HER OR THE
                                BLACK REVOLUTION IS DEAD
    . . . . AND DONT START TELLING ME WHAT   Y O U
                                AINT   GOT!!

SCENERY

the flowers are dead
the vase is broken
water leaked out   drowned a family
of roaches
they are gone   the table is bare   toilet dont flush
fleas/rats/mice/ and dead roaches
legions of bandit bed bugs   called chinches   patrol
the rock'n'roll squeaky sex bed
everywhere   flowers   are dead
vases are broke   like maiden head   on a roof
slumlord's   throat   slashed   as expected   like a
                              punchline of a black joke

BREAD

Money is the world! Dollars/Francs/Marks/Kronor/
Pesetas/Guilder/Rupees/Pounds/Pounds/Escudos/ Drachmas/
etc etc   Money is your mother/money is your father/money
is your entire family/all your living and dead relatives
mean money/money is your god/money is your god/money is your
god/money is your god/money is your god/your goal is money/
your interest is money/you will cheat to get money/you
will steal to get money/you have always killed to get money/
you have always killed to get money/you have always killed to
get money/you have always killed to get money/you will sell
your soul (if you had one!) for money/you are always looking
for new ways to make more money/you can not have your power
without money/your minutes and years are lived for money/in
the beginning of your life the word was . . . .

33

A FEW BLUE WORDS TO THE WISE

to   SHOUT/ RAVE / RANT/   and RAGE   is being militant as
                                           hell but not very brave
        (Especially when you're before an all Black audience)

to   SCREAM/ SNEER / BELLOW/ and even fart   is being
                                           excited/worked-up but
        all that wont stop a Honky heart

to curse/ and call him names (all true) is not really bad   Yet it
                                           makes our black
        poetry look sad (You know,like we aint got nothing better to
                                           poet about)

Then: or thus:
We must write poems black brothers about our own black relations
We must fall in love and glorify our beautiful black nation
We must create black images   give the world
     a black education

OPEN MINDED

She opened her eyes   and she saw me
She opened her ears   and she heard my words
She opened her nose   and smelled the truth
She opened her dress and revealed body and soul
She opened her arms   and I knew her need
She laid back/opened her legs,opened her heart,   and separated her
lonely knees   Yes indeed Yes Indeed   Yeeessss INDEED!   **35**

DUKE'S ADVICE

I live Uptown in Harlem   I took Duke's advice
and took the "A" Train   Now I'm surrounded by my tribe again
                                                     in Harlem
    I sleep in bed between two dream queens black   naked women
                                                     in Harlem
    I dream this same dream every night Uptown "A" Trainland
                                                     in Harlem
  What I'm trying to not say   is Uptown I have erotic dreams
                                                     it seems about
    Bessie Smith and Billie Holiday   When I close my eyes they
                                                     stay and we lay
    Uptown   in "A" Trainland in a big black bed in Harlem

UNCLE TOM TOM

UNCLE TOM TOM CAME A RUNNING   WITH $ GOVERNMENT
                GRANTS BRITISH ACCENT & AWFUL LOT OF
                MISINFORMATION ABOUT BLACK AFRICA
                AND AMERICA (BLACK IS WHAT THIS NEGRO
                DID LACK)
UNCLE TOM TOM WAS WELCOMED BY WHITE BUSINESS
                VULTURES & THEIR BLACK HYENA LACKEYS
                WHO ROBBED & RAPED   AFRICA'S NAKED
                BODY
UNCLE TOM TOM FOOLED HIMSELF   FOOLED HIS RULERS
                AND PLAYED HIS FOOLISH ROLE OF
                INDIVIDUAL NEGRO U.S.A. WITH HIS U.S.I.S.
                PLUS I.B.M. MESSED UP SOUL
UNCLE TOM TOM TRAVELS JET   SLEEPS AIR CONDITIONED
                AND KNOWS ALL IMPERIALIST SERPENTS BY
                THEIR FIRST NAMES AND THEIR WIVES BY SEX
                & DRINK   THEY ALL JUST ADORE THIS NICE
                COLORED MAN   AMBITIOUS UNCLE   TOM
                TOM   WITH HIS INTERNATIONAL ATTACHE
                CASE
                we must see that
                    Uncle Tom Tom
                        dies soon for the
                            white race

REVENGE

WITH OPEN KNIFE HE WALKED THE STREETS
LIKE AN AWFUL SINGLE FANG SNAKE
   WITH   CLOUDED MIND HE TALKED IN SNEERS
AS THOUGH THE ENEMY WAS DIGGING HIM ON T.V.
  WITH TORN SHIRT FILLED WITH HURT HE LOOKED MEAN
WORSE THAN RAINY PICNIC PARK GROUNDS
  WHERE HIS OPPONENT HAD GIVEN THE BEATING
LIKE A STAMPEDE OF THIRSTY CAMELS
  WITH BRUISES AND WOUNDED PRIDE OF DEFEAT
LIKE   A MOVIE HERO RUNNING ALL THE WAY HOME
TO GET THE REVENGING SHARP BLADE KNIFE
  LIKE AN AWFUL MEAN DRAB GOD
HE INTENDS TO STAB OUT HIS OPPONENT'S LIFE

NOT YET UHURU

YOU'RE BLACK BUT NOT YET BEAUTIFUL
CAUSE YOUR OLD INSIDES AINT STRAIGHT
YOU'RE BEAUTIFUL BUT STILL A N E G R O
CAUSE WHITE WASH DONT RUB OFF   EASY
YOU'RE HIP   BUT AINT NO WHERE
CAUSE YOU DONT COME ON ACTIVELY
YOU KNOW WHERE ITS AT, YET WONT TURN ME ON
YOU'RE FULLA SOUL BUT COME ON ALL COLD
AND YOU KNOW THAT AINT *IT*
SO BABY
            I'M GONNA TELL EVERYBODY
                            YOU AINT SHIT!

FOR ME AGAIN

I'VE SEEN MY MOTHER AGAIN   MORE YEARS THAN TEN
                                      HAVE PASSED BY
SHE STILL FAT LIKE THE SUN   COOKING OLD SMELLY SOUL
                                 FOODS   FOR ME AGAIN
MORE YEARS THAN TEN HAVE PASSED US BY   SEEING/HEARING/
                                 FEELING/ SILENTLY TOGETHER
WE CRY MY MOTHER AND I   She still wise and warm   for me again
This woman/ my mother   This woman/ MY FRIEND   39

WATERMELON

Its got   a good shape/the outside color is green/its one of them
        foods from Africa
its got stripes sometimes like a zebra   or Florida prison pants
Its bright red inside/the black eyes are flat and shiney/it wont make
        you fat
Its got heavy liquid weight/the sweet taste is unique/some people are
        shamed of it/
I aint afraid to eat it/indoors or out/its soul food thing/Watermelon
        is what I'm
talking about   Yeah watermelon is what I'm talking about
        Watermelon

PRICKUNTIDY

Obo   is open like a cowrie

Oku   is hard and wishes to hide

Obo   is wide spread like sky

Oku   shall rush around inside   spit life   against the Obo insides   41

DEMYSTIFY

Dont send me black mail/ for I am black male/thus I black ball/
WOMEN/ not black sheep/and never black out/awake or sleep/ I,
black male/hold black magic secrets/unintegrated thus un-
twisted/ Whites have black male/ as I/ delivered censored/ or
black listed/I the black male

42

WHO TO?

Send letters to

colored people &

they'll write white

b a c k   43

PROMISED LAND

LANGSTON HUGHES
PAID HIS DUES
IN THE HARLEMS
OF   THE U.S.A.
HE
POETED THE
POLLUTED

MAKING PROSE
TO ZOOT SUITED
THUS TOLD WHAT
THE NEGRO
HAD TO SAY
LANGSTON HUGHES
NEVER BLEW HIS COOL
NOR DID HE
SIDE   WITH
the "MAN"
HIS STORIES,PLAYS, &
PROSE
& HIS BLACK POETRY
SHOWS
N I G G E R S CANT
WAIT
FOR NO
"PROMISED LAND"

START LOVING

I LOVE   YOU
THAT I'M CERTAIN
I AM THE WINDOW
AND YOU'RE MY CURTAIN
YET YOU ARE NOT POSITIVE
ON GIVING ME YOUR HEART
BUT I STILL LOVE YOU
UNTIL   YOU   START

YEAHH I DIG

you're suppose to be hip
Yeah I know
when you see a black cat with a fay chick
you dont flip
Yeah I dig
you're suppose to be avant garde
Yeah I know
when LeRoi/Rap/Stokely/ blow truth
you dont find them too hard
Yeah I dig
Yeah I dig
some of your BEST friends are 'Negroes'
you entertain them at your parties until the last white guest goes
Yeah I dig
you were in the Civil Rights bag long long time down south ago
Yeah I dig
you know all about spades and you want to help them so
Yeah I dig
Yeah I dig
but what I dont dig
is why do you refuse   and   frown
when I tell you to take up a gun like your own white John Brown
or why do you get uptight or copout funny
when ever I mention   giving me some money??
Yeah I dig
Yeah I really do dig!!

AFRICA

to Abu Ansar

Africa
  A free continent
  A -FRI -CA
  A free continent
A free con ti nent
a fri ca
a fri ca
a fri ca
a free continent
a f r i c a
a free continent
ALGERIA*/ BURUNDI/ CAMEROUN/
CENTRAL AFRICAN REPUBLIC/CHAD/ Congo/
Kinshasha & Brazzaville*/ Dahomey/ Ethiopia/ Gabon/
Gambia/ Ghana/ Guinea*/ Ivory Coast/ Liberia/ Libya/
Madagascar/ Malawi/ Mali*/ Mauritania/ Morocco/ Niger/
Nigeria/ Rwanda/ Senegal/ Sierra Leone/ Somalia/ Sudan/
Tanzania*/ Togo/ Tunisia/ Uganda/ United Arab Republic*/
Upper Volta/ Zambia*/
A FREE CONTINENT
          A FRI CA
              A   FREE CO NTINENT
                              A FRI CA
          AFRICA
    A FREE CONTINENT
                to-be to-be to-be

ON RUE JACQUES CALLOT

on rue Jacques Callot in Paris
a girl watches a man's pants fall
the sun flips like a tossed coin
and the girl licks her lips slow
on rue Jacques Callot in France

on   this sunnyside street in Paris
a black flower first saw a Man Ray
and last saw Le Verre d'eau dans la Tempête
the naked beard makes sounds of dogs barking
on the rue Jacques Callot inParis

on the rue Jacques Callot in Europe
where   exquisite corpses drink no wines
the moon is pregnant with loud poems
and young whores knees lock against fever
on the rue Jacques Callot in France

on Rue Jacques Callot on Left Bank
a flame thrower gives a taxi pillow
the water melon eater sucks a pussy cat
and four velvet pairs of panties swear
on the Rue Jacques Callot in the Paris

MY BAG

to Cecil Taylor

MY BAG   IS HERE   IT IS JUST MY SIZE
MY BAG IS DEEP   AND DARK   SO DONT
BE TOO SMART   I   HAVE MY BAG
IT IS ALL MY OWN   AND I   AND I ALONE
KNOWS WHAT IS HAPPENING IN MY BAG
MY BAG IS WARM   SOMETIMES HOT BUT HIP
MY BAG IS   NOTHING MORE THAN MY BAG
THUS IT MAY JUST BE TOO DAMN HEAVY
FOR YOU TO WORRY OR TRY TO CARRY   BUT
DONT GET UPSET AND SCARY   ITS MY BAG
I KNOW MY BAG   CAUSE IT IS MY BAG
I KNOW EXACTLY WHERE ITS AT   MY BAG

48

WHY ELSE?

to my first son Ted Nkrumah

I FELL IN LOVE   WITH A VERY STRANGE GUY
HE HAD   TWO EARS   TWO EYES   TWO ARMS
TWO HANDS   TWO LIPS   TWO LEGS
TWO THUMBS   TWO ELBOWS
AND JUST   TWO FEET   TALL
BUT THEY   WOULDNT LET ME   LOVE HIM
IN AMERICA   BECAUSE   HE WAS   MY SON
AND   JUST HAPPEN   TO BE   BORN
TOO   WHITE!

SALUTE TO THE SAHARA

Sahara I have crossed you
with four litres of water
oriental patience and
ancestral spiritual guidance
I dreamed I had two Swiss cooks
who pushed a Volkswagen bus
across your vast seas of sand and rock
I salute you Sahara   you've always frightened
Western man   who thinks you're nothing but an
ocean of sand   I know what you are I've traveled you
triple sunsets/more welcome dawns/hot high noons
You are a big brown woman with legs spread wide
waiting for the masculine and brave to come inside
I salute you Sahara   the mighty/the dangerous/Sahara

BARE BEAUTY

she is naked now
nudity is her golden gown
no clothing at all
protects   and hides
her delicate black
body   although
she wears a smile
on her lovely face
   and down there some-
where is a forest
from there and nowhere
else comes the increases
of our race

TAKEN CARE OF BUSINESS

TAKE CARE OF BUSINESS
BLACK BUSINESS
ITS ALL OURS
NOT ON C.P.TIME
BUT B.P. TIME
ITS OUR TIME
TO TAKE CARE OF BUSINESS
BLACK BUSINESS
IN OUR OWN SWEET WAY
BEING ON BLACK TIME
TAKING CARE OF BUSINESS
EVERY BLACK NIGHT
AND EVERY BLACK DAY
DOING WHAT HAS TO BE DONE
TOGETHER AS ONE
NOW   WITH NO C.P.TIME DELAY

HE SPY

cop   concealed   in   our group
calling us brothers &
putting   whitey   down by
calling it mother
police plant on our scene
asking questions
listening to black plans
collecting data
only for the MAN
nappy fuzz infiltrator
skin color is grey
afro dressed trying
to disguise his white
affiliation   he believes
in money/integration or
dropping on China   the bomb
SICK NIGGER   THIS UNCLE PEEPING   TOM!

51

Telephone Book

NEITHER LIFE/TIME/EBONY/ or   LOOK

you are just telephone book

you're heavy   and   fat

weighs a young ton or more

telephone book

you're flabby   and square

your print like wrinkles

old over weight bulky

telephone book

clumsy yellowed pages

making searching eyes grow sore
        WHO needs your listings
            YOU   WHO   TELL - A -PHONE - BOOK NOTHING

NATURAL

thick lips/ natural
wide nose/ natural
kinky hair/ natural
brown eyes / natural
w i d e   s m i l e / natural
black skin/natural
& if you're proud/of what you
naturally got
then your soul/is beautiful/thus
naturally hot   so be natural
stay natural   swing natural   think natural
and for black god's sake   act   natural

SANTA CLAWS

IF THAT WHITE MOTHER HUBBARD COMES DOWN MY BLACK
    CHIMNEY   DRAGGING HIS PLAYFUL BAG
IF THAT RED SUITED FAGGOT STARTS HO HO HOING ON MY
    ROOFTOP
IF THAT OLD FAT CRACKERCREEPS INTO MY HOUSE
IF THAT ANTIQUE REINDEER RAPER RACES ACROSS MY LAWN
IF THAT OLD TIME NIGGER KNOCKER FILLS MY WIFE'S STOCKING
IF THAT HAINT WHO THINKS HE'S A SAINT
COMES SLED FLYING ACROSS MY HOME
IF THAT OLD CON MAN COMES ON WITH HIS TOYFUL JIVE
IF THAT OVER STUFFED GUT BUSTING GANGSTER
    SHOWS UP TONIGHT
HE AND ME SHOW GONNA HAVE A BATTLING XMAS AND IT SHOW
    AINT GONNA BE WHITE!

THEY BLACK AS BLACK ME   THEY DIG BLACK ART
(FOR FREE)

to Harlem's Art Galleries

they black as black me   they dig black art(for free)
they buy good clothes   buy materials   and buy each year a new car
they black as black me   but they turn a shade of grey   when they
    have to pay for
black as black me   who happens to be   the   black   artist   55

YOU BLACK . . . . . .

IF   THEY'D   CALL   US   BLACK   OR   WE'D   CALL US   BLACK

JUST   A FEW   YEARS   AGO   BACK   I'M PRETTY SURE   WE'D
    KNOCK'EM DOWN

BEAT'EM UP   OR KICK'EM AROUND   IF THEY'D   CALLED   US
    BLACK WAY BACK THEN

ON BEING IN LOVE

to P.J. from T.J.

I'M IN LOVE   DEEPLY IN LOVE   COVERD IN LOVE

INSIDE & OUTSIDE IN LOVE   AND SHE'S IN LOVE

DEEPLY IN LOVE   COVERD IN LOVE   ALL HER TIME   IN

LOVE   IN   LOVE IN   LOVE   IN LOVE   IN   LOVE   WITH ME

COLD WEATHER CAUSES   CURSES

COLD WEATHER CAUSES   CURSES   TO SPRING FORTH FROM
   WARM HEARTED MOUTHS

COLD WEATHER CAUSES BLACK ME AND BLACK YOU TO DISAGREE
   EVEN TO THE BROKEN BRIDGES

OF IGNORING EACH OTHER   SISTER ARGUING WITH BROTHER
   FATHER BATTLING MOTHER

COLD WEATHER CAUSES OUR HOT BODIES TO GROW OLD AND
   DISEASED   COLD WEATHER IS

THE NUMBER TWO ENEMY   (SNEEZE!!)

THERE ARE THOSE

There are those that say   that people are people   music is music
    and dues are dues
and theres no different between night and day   These are the ones
    that cant sing blues
There are those that say   that   they have it just as bad as blacks
    that *they too* pay dues!
and theres no different between night and day   These are the ones
    that cant sing blues
But for these people anyway   crime does pay

STORMY MONDAY GIRLS

THEY ALL CAME OUT THAT STORMY MONDAY
WHITE BOYS THAT COLLECTED   JAZZ
                                    RECORDINGS
WHITE MEN THAT WROTE ABOUT JAZZ
                                    PLAYERS
WHITE MIDDLE AGED MARRIED COUPLES WHO
                    DANCED TO JAZZ
AND OF COURSE WHITE WOMEN THAT
        COLLECTED BLACK JAZZ MUSICIANS AT
THESE STORMY MONDAY EVENING SESSIONS
                                    WHERE
WHITE BOYS SAT AND LISTENED TO EVERY
                                    NOTE
AND WHITE MEN WHO EARNED THEIR SALARY
                    BY WHAT THEY WROTE
AND WHITE MIDDLE AGED COUPLES DANCING
                    WITHOUT THEIR COATS
AND   OF COURSE   MISS ANN WHO
            KNEW EVERY BLACK CAT
IN THE BAND   SHE WOULD SOMETIMES TAKE THE BLACK JAZZ
                                    BEST TO HER
HIP PAD,TENDER TRAP OF CONTAGIOUS CLAPP (HER CROW
                                    JIM NEST?)
AND ALL THE WHILE WHITE BOYS DUG JAZZ LIKE BEING
                                    IN SCHOOL
AND WHITE MEN TOOK DOWN CRITICAL NOTES AND INTERVIEWED
AND WHITE MIDDLE AGED COUPLES WENT HOME EARLY
                                    (TO SCREW!)
MISS HIPPER-THAN-THOU (THE UBIQUITOUS COW!) WHO ALL BLACK
                                    JAZZMEN
KNEW   SHE TURNED THE TABLES ON THE BLACK JAZZ CATS
AND CUT OUT WITH AN ENGLISH JAZZ JEW!

CHANGED

HIS FEET   WERE   BAD/bad'er than HE WAS
HIS FISTS WERE   HARD/harder than HE WAS
HIS WORK WAS T O U G H/but HE WAS tougher
HIS   LIFE WAS R O U G H/ but HE WAS rougher
HIS   TALK   was hip/but he was wiser
HIS FACE WAS BLACK/but his SOUL was blacker
SHE ANGERED H I M/but   he   refused to abuse and smacker
HE WAS A BLACK MAN THE WIFE BEATING negro HAD
                              LONG-GONE from his soul

60

THE NON-JOHN BROWNS

LOVE OF FREEDOM   IS WHY THE   THIRD   WORLD FIGHTS
NO PEACE   NO   REST   NO   COMPROMISE   FOR THE
THIRD   WORLD'S   ENEMY   WHOM IS: the non-john brown
  WHITES   WHO WILL NOT TAKE UP GUNS AND FIGHT
                              AGAINST THEIR KITH & KIN
NO   PEACE   NO REST   NO COMPROMISES
FROM MORNINGS TIL NOONS THRU NIGHTS OF BLACK
   SURPRISES!
LOVE OF FREEDOM   IS WHY THE   THIRD   WORLD   U N I T E S
NO PEACE   NO REST   NO COMPROMISE   FOR   THE
                                   THIRD WORLD'S
ENEMY: THE   NON-JOHN BROWN   WHITES

BEAUTY

BEAUTY IS NOT FOUND IN ONE'S FACE / NOR IN THE
        NATIONALITY OR THE RACE
        NO NO WORLD   BEAUTY IS THE SOUL

BEAUTY IS NOT THE DORIS DAY GLITTER / NOR IS IT SAMMY
        DAVIS THAT MAKES YOU TWITTER
        NO NO WORLD   BEAUTY IS THE SOUL

62   BEAUTY IS NOT THE BLOODY CRY IN BATTLE / NOR IS IT THE
        SLAUGHTER OF BULL FIGHTER'S CATTLE
        NO NO WORLD   BEAUTY IS THE SOUL

BEAUTY IS NOT THE WEIGHT OF MONEY / NOR IS IT A SEXACT
        WITH A PLAYBOY BUNNY
        NO NO WORLD   BEAUTY IS THE SOUL

BEAUTY IS NOT OWNED BY JUST ONE PERSON / NOR IS IT
        CONFINED TO RELIGIOUS WORDS OR CURSING
        NO NO WORLD   BEAUTY IS THE SOUL

BEAUTY IS NOT THE PAINTING THAT LOOKS SO "for real" / NOR IS
        IT IS A CORNY RHYMING POETIC DEAL
        (so I shall SHUT UP world) CAUSE

        BEAUTY IS THE SOUL

THE VILLAGE VOICE

You   and you
and I do mean   Y O U
and even   YOU   too
allyall   my enemies! !
until   you
and you
and I do mean YOU
and even   YOU   too (who tried to remove it)
ALLYALL   MY   ENEMY
UNTIL   ALLYALL   CAN   PROVE   IT!!!

SHUT UP SUSTAH!!

SHE SPOKE OUT AGAINST A BROTHER
SHE PUT HIM DOWN   WAYDOWN   BELOW
SHE SCREAMED ON A TRUE BLOOD
SHE SHOUTED ABUSE AT A DARK DADDY
SHE TALKED ABOUT HIM HARD THAT NIGHT
THE WAY SHE FELT   WAS HER   RIGHT
YET SHE WAS WRONG   BECAUSE THE AUDIENCE WAS WHITE
SHUT UP SUSTAH   SHUT UP

64

BLACK FEBRUARY BLOOD LETTING

L U M U M B A   WAS MURDERED AND MADE A MARTYR
                               IN THE MONTH

OF FEBRUARY   BUT no dish broke in sink of the UN-UNITED
                                  NATIONS

M A L C O L M X WAS MURDERED AND MADE A HERO IN
                         FEBRUARY AND STILL

YET NO ELECTRIC COUCH HAS GAVE BIRTH TO A HIGH
                             VOLTAGE HUM

A B U B A K A   T A F A W A   B A L I W E L A   WAS FOUND
                              DEAD IN HIS OWN
FEBRUARY NIGERIA ALTHOUGH no witch doctor raised a bone
                               toward Mecca

K W A M E   N K R U M A H WAS DETHRONED IN HIS ABSENCE
                              IN THE

G H A N A   FEBRUARY   AND STILL YET I CAN NOT FORGET
                             that not one:

   CHINESE RED   RUSSIAN RED   OR ANY OTHER
                             KINDA RED

   DID ANYTHING MILITANTLY TO HONOR THESE BLACK
                           FEBRUARY DEAD

GIT IT!

to Walter Rodney

BUY IT
STEAL IT
TAKE IT
TRY IT
KNOW IT
LOAD IT
USE IT
and make the ENEMY   DIE of IT!

THE WHITE BAN

BAN THE SPEARS,ARROWS,AND CLUBS   THEY WHISPERED OVER
   WHITE BIBLES

AND WE DID IT   THEN THEY ENSLAVED US WITH THEIR GUNS

BAN THE RIFLES,CANNONS, AND REVOLVERS   THEY SHOUT
THROUGH WHITE   declarations of white LAW & ORDER   and we did it
THEY further enslave us   with their BOMBS   67

Now they scream "BAN THE BOMBS!" "STOP ITS SPREAD!"

WHAT THEY REALLY WANT   IS BAN US   GENOCIDE   THEY WANT US
               ENSLAVED   OR   DEAD
                    N E V E R   S A Y   N O

UNTOO

DO UNTO   WHITE OTHERS   as they do

UNTO   OUR THIRD WORLD BROTHERS

WALLS

LISTEN TO THE SOUL SOUNDS THROUGH PAPER THIN WALLS
LISTEN TO THE LOVERS HOT JULY SLAPPED THIGH,SEXUAL SIGH
   THROUGH THE WALLS
LISTEN TO THE LOW MOAN,THE SUGGESTIVE GROAN, . . . AND
   SQUEAKING BED
NUFF NOISE COMING OUTTA THERE   TO RAISE THE DEAD
LISTEN TO SOUL SOUNDS COMING THROUGH THE WALLS . . . . . .

68   CANT YALL HEAR IT??

WINTER HAWK IN HARLEM

HE WORE CLEAN WHITE   COTTON CLOTH PANTS
HIS   AFRO HAIR-DO   WAS CROWNED BY   ISLAMIC SILK CAP
HIS EXPRESSION MILITANT   SO WAS HIS   STANCE
HIS CREDENTIALS WERE SOLID   BLACK
BUT HIS CLOTHING   WAS   VERY   UNCOOL
FOR THE   HAWK   HAD   ARRIVED
IN   HARLEM   THUS   PNEUMONING THIS
SANDAL WEARING   BLACK   FOOL   69

MANUFACTURELATION

THEY WHITE

        & THEY ALWAYS SAY: MAKE money/ MAKE
        coffee/ MAKE movie/ MAKE tea/

        MAKE music/ MAKE gun/ MAKE war/ MAKE fun/
        MAKE car/ MAKE art/

        MAKE bed/ and THEY E V E N make L O V E
        but NOT to ME

        because I'm a spade & can NOT be made

JAZZ IS MY RELIGION

JAZZ is my religion   and it alone do I dig   the jazz clubs are
my houses of worship   and sometimes the concert halls   but some
holy places are too commercial (like churches)   so I dont dig the
sermons there   I buy jazz sides to dig in solitude   Like man/Harlem,
Harlem U.S.A. used to be a jazz heaven where most of the jazz
sermons were preached   but now-a-days due to chacha cha and
rotten rock'n'roll alotta good jazzmen have sold their souls   but jazz
is still my religion   because I know and feel the message it brings
like Reverend Dizzy Gillespie/ Brother   Bird and Basie/ Uncle
Armstrong/ Minster Monk/ Deacon Miles Davis/ Rector Rollins/
Priest Ellington/ His Funkness Horace Silver/ and the great Pope
John,John COLTRANE   and Cecil Taylor   They Preach A Sermon
That Always Swings!!   Yeah jazz is MY religion   Jazz is my story
it was my mom's and pop's   and their moms and pops from the
days of Buddy Bolden who swung them blues to Charlie Parker and
Ornette Coleman's extension of Bebop   Yeah jazz is my religion
Jazz is a unique musical religion   the sermons spread happiness and
joy   to be able to dig and swing inside   what a wonderful feeling
jazz is/YEAH BOY!!   JAZZ is my religion and dig this: it wasnt for
us to choose because they created it for a damn good reason   as a
weapon to battle our blues! JAZZ is my religion   and its
international   all the   way   JAZZ is just an Afroamerican music⁕
and like us its here to stay   So remember that JAZZ is my religion
but it can be your religion too but JAZZ is a truth that   is always
black and blue   Hallelujah I love JAZZ so   Hallelujah I dig JAZZ so
Yeah J A Z Z   I S   M Y   R E L I G I O N

NO MORE

I love her black butt
the way it moves   when she walks
I dig her natural lips   unpainted/full/ & soft
I adore her dark eyes
they way they flash   when she lets go
I dig sister soul   but she dont want me   no more

LIKE ME

They ask: what is Africa like? I tell them: Africa is like me! Black/

Big/ complex/ creative/ magic/undeveloped wealth/ and not yet free

ME TOO!

HE HAS GONE TOO FAR . . . .

HE IS   NOW   TOO EXTREME . . . . . .

HE IS   REALLY   IRRESPONSIBLE

74   THOSE   BLACK CATS   THAT DESTROY   THE
AMERICAN DREAM!!!

BLACK PEOPLE

I SEE BLACK PEOPLE
I HEAR BLACK PEOPLE
I SMELL BLACK PEOPLE
I TASTE BLACK PEOPLE
I TOUCH BLACK PEOPLE
BLACK PEOPLE IS MY MOMMA
BLACK PEOPLE IS MY DAD
BLACK PEOPLE IS   MY SISTER,BROTHER,UNCLE,AUNT,AND COUSINS
BLACK PEOPLE IS   ALL WE   BLACK PEOPLE   EVER HAD
NOW THAT WE THE BLACK PEOPLE KNOW THAT
WE THE BLACK PEOPLE SHOULD BE GLAD

JAZZ MUST BE A WOMAN

to all the jazzmen that I fail to include

Jazz must be a woman because its the only thing that
Albert Ayler Albert Ammons Albert Nichols Gene Ammons Cat
Anderson Louis Armstrong Buddy Bolden Ornette Coleman Buster
Bailey Ben Bailey Benny Harris Ben Webster Beaver Harris Alan
Shorter Coleman Hawkins Count Basie Dave Bailey Dexter Gordon
Danny Barker Wayne Shorter Duke Ellington Jay Macshann Earl
Hines Tiny Grimes Barney Bigard Sahib Shihab Sid Catlett jelly roll
Morton Nat King Cole Johnny Coles Lee Collins John Collins Sonny
Rollins Pete Brown Jay Jay Johnson Dickie Wells Vic Dickenson Ray
Nance Junior Mance Sonny Parker Charlie Parker Leo Parker Lee
Morgan Mal Waldron Ramsey Lewis John Lewis George Lewis Pops
Foster Curtiss Fuller Jimmie Cleveland Billy Higgins John Coltrane
Cozy Cole Bill Coleman Idries Sulimann Hank Mobley Charlie
Mingus Dizzy Gillespie Lester Young Harney Carney Cecil Payne
Sonny Payne Roy Haynes Max Roach Thelonious Monk Wes
Montgomery Johnny Dodds Johnny Hodges Kenny Drew Kenny
Durham Ernie Wilkins Ernie Royal Babs Gonzales McCoy Tyner
Clifford Brown Shadow Wilson Teddy Wilson Gerald Wilson Wynton
Kelly Huddie Leadbelly Big Bill Bronzy Cannonball Adderly Bobbie
Timmons Sidney Bechet Sonny Criss Sonny Stitt Fats Navarro Ray
Charles Benny Carter Lawrence Brown Ray Brown Charlie Moffett
Sonny Murray Milt Buckner Milt Jackson Miles Davis Horace Silver
Bud Powell Kenny Burrell Teddy Bunn Teddy Buckner King Oliver
Oliver Nelson Tricky Sam Nanton Buber Miley Freddy Webster
Freddy Redd Benny Green Jackie Maclean Art Simmins Art Blakey
Art Taylor Cecil Taylor Billy Taylor Gene Taylor Clark Terry Don
Cherry Sonny Terry Joe Turner Joe Thomas Ray Bryant Freddie
Greene Freddie Hubbard Donald Byrd Roland Kirk Carl Perkins
Morris Lane Harry Edison Percey Heath Jimmy Heath Jimmy Smith
Willie Smith Buster Smith Floyd Smith Johnny Smith Pinetop Smith
Stuff Smith Tab Smith Willie 'the Lion' Smith Roy Eldridge Charlie
Shavers Eddie South Les Spann Les Macann Speckled Red Eddie
Vinson Mr. Cleanhead Rex Stewart Slam Stewart Art Tatum Erskine
Hawkins Cootie Williams Lionel Hampton Ted Curson John Tchicai

Joe Thomas Lucky Thompson Sir Charles Thompson T-Bone Walker
Fats Waller Julius Watkins Doug Watkins Muddy Waters Washboard
Sam Memphis Slim Leo Watson Chick Webb Frank Wess Denzil Best
Randy Weston Clarence Williams Joe Williams Rubberlegs Williams
Spencer Williams Sonnyboy Williams Tampa Red Jimmy
Witherspoon Britt Woodman Leo Wright Jimmy Yancey Trummy
Young Snooky Young James P Johnson Bunk Johnson Budd
Johnson Red Garland Erroll Garner Jimmy Garrison Matthew Gee
Cecil Gant Walter Fuller Roosevelt Sykes Slim Gaillard Harold Land
Pete Laroca Yusef Lateef Billy Kyle John Kirby Al Killian Andy Kirk
Freddie Keppard Taft Jordan Duke Jordon Louis Jordan Cliff
Jordan Scott Joplin Willie Jones Wallace Jones Sam Jones Rejnald
Jones Quincy Jones Philly Jo Jones Jimmy Jones Hank Jones Elvin
Jones Ed jones Claude Jones Rufus Jones Curtiss Jones Richard
Jones Wilore 'slick' Jones Thad Jones and of course me . . . . . TED
JOANS/ yes JAZZ must be a WOMAN because its the only thing
that we Jazzmen want to . . . . B L O W !!

ITS CURTAINS

All god's SPADES wear dark shades
    and some of god's SPADES
(you'll never be able to figger what nigger)
      carry l   o   n   g   sharp

        protective blades
                     so I repeat, though
78   he may be raggedy or neat
      All god's SPADES got SHADES

WHY TRY?

And she was brown
And she always dressed and wore brown
And she had a fine brown body body
And she had two beautiful brown eyes
And she would sit in the Beat Cafe
on her brown behind on a hard brown bench
and listen to brown sounds entertain her brown thoughts

And she would often double cross her big brown legs
And reveal her beautiful brown pleasing knees
And as she sat in the Beat Cafe on her brown behind on the hard
    brown bench
And listening to brown sounds coming from brown entertainers of
    brown bohemia
I   saw   a young white girl   throw away her brand
    new jar of
            suntan lotion and sigh: WHY TRY?

THE OVER LOADED HORSE

On a battu le cheval, au mois de Mai and they ate him
his buttons were crushed into powder for their soup
   his hair was wovened into ship sails
his foreskin was sewn by an antique dealer
his manure supplied several generations with xmas gifts
   and now they speak bad of him,the horse,the head of their family
   On a battu le cheval, au mois de Mai and they ate him
   his earwax was packaged in America
his rump was displayed on early morning garbage trucks
   his crossed eye is on loan to a soap museum
   his manners have since been copied by millions of glass blowers
   and still yet, they spit at his stable,the horse,the head of the house
   On a battu le cheval, au mois de Mai and they ate him
his ribs were riveted outside an airbase
his knees bend in shadows of Russia
   his shoelaces are used to hang lonely violinists
his dignity is exported as a dairy product to the Orient
   and in spite of it all, those he loved most,lie and cheat horse's heirs
   On a battu le cheval, au mois de Mai and they ate him
   his tears now drown the frowning yachtsmen
his urine flows rapidly across millionaires estates
his annual vomit destroys twelve dictators promises a year
his teeth tear wide holes in the scissor maker's Swiss bank account
   and even in death,filled with revenge,they eat him again and again,
   they deny   and lie as they speak bad of the horse,the head of their
   house, the father of their home

S.C. THREW S.C. INTO THE RAILROAD YARD

to Stokely who threw it away on that day

It is crystal clear
He threw it away   He shoved it into the sky He tossed it away
like an old dry piece of shit
He pushed it up   high   into the space thrust it up there with the
    strength of a million winged black bird
He got rid of it   He lost it from his neck for ever He shed it in the
    filthy Chalk air over the boring Dialectic farm
He made it go far away   he caused the distance to grow as it soared
It is gone it is dead it is no more   the sky trap has claimed it
He has got his own
from his own sent to him by his own   He is longer alone or wearing
    borrowed bits
He has a gri-gri of his own   It has freed him from St Christopher's
    medal
He is no longer under the spell of false god/A white man's medal-god
    worn also by the three astronauts who fried in Florida's famous
    event
The medal no longer hangs from his black neck
He has a gri-gri of his own   made of spiritual materials   living
    elements
Gri-gri from Africa   black magic to do great harm to his oppressors
gri-gri to give him strength and wisdom   Growing stronger
    encircling his
body   just around his neck   below his handsome black head
His Bambara face   His Nilotic frame   His Ashanti majesty   His
    Hipness of Harlem
He has thrown the white medal of St Christopher away
He is now free   from the money Man's bit   He no longer sucks Holy
    Mary's tit
He has a gri-gri of his own
A black gri-gri
a grinning cunt shaped cowrie shell gri-gri
a brown black blue leather breathing amulet gri-gri
brought from the black sorceror
across the Sahara   across the Atlantic and Mediterranean
from black Africa   by me

SPARE THE FLIES BUT KILL THE LIES

to the Flower Power Hippies

Timbuctu? they snigger in London
"Father told me there is no such place"
Timbuctoo had universities and commerce
"Mother said, Africans are the uncivilised race"
Timbuktu is older than Paris or London
"Uncle Jock said, Arab historians told lies"
Timbucto is located in northern Mali
"Aunt Elizabeth says, it's where camels go when they die"
Timbuktoo, I'm telling you
Peopled by blacks, browns and Tuareg men of blue,
desert town, running water, electric light
Twice a week (if you're chic) tourist plane flight
So when your Kith and Kin speak of Africa or Timbuctu
It's just bloody imperialist lies
that they continue telling you

BLACK LIGHT

It is crystal clear

It is crystal clear to me

It is crystal clear to you

It is crystal clear to them

It is crystal clear to some

It is crystal clear to those

It is crystal clear to these

that we blacks, no longer, want to please

I AM HUNGRY

I am hurting because
I am hungry
I am sweating & eyes
are pissing down
my hungry face &
I am feeling sad
I am so hungry
I am nervous &
angry with all
I am hungry &
what I need
is someone
to feed me
some love

THE FIRE NEXT TIME BLUES

you put me down   when I needed you most
you kicked me out   you were a very rude host
you maltreated me
I'll give you the fire next time

you mistreated me/ rejected me/ threatened me/ &
economically enslaved poor me
but I've got MY bag
I'll give you the fire next time

you ignored/floored/ became bored/
you cheated/taunted/ became conceited/
you exploited me
I'll give you the fire next time

I hate you, Wow!! You taught me how/so I'll give you the fire
            R ight N ow!!!

NEVER

to L.J. from T.J.

In French the king is

called Le Roi/in Memphis
theysaid the king was
dead/shot by white in the
head   In my mind the king
still lives   to destroy white
louse   Le Roi Vive le Roi

The king lives in Spirit house

COLORED CHORUSES

in memory of Bob Thompson

in the window   i saw
the last tear drop fall
crushing a red rose green
glass blades sprinkled
with light white drops
of dew said goodbye mid
night and hello morning blues!

trying hard to get it
inside (white muse and zem!)
where goodtimes roll
all night'n'day long
crying loud (white muse)
to let you know that
I'm (zem) sorry I done
you w r o n g!!

many mother many mothers
point toward others other
and show where the real
truth lies and cries
lies and cries hard
times come fast(if we
last)now that other
many mother satisfies

blow your horn black daddy
scream on the mother for real!
blow your horn black daddy
dont smile   clown   or dance
just
blow your horn black daddy!!

when i saw your face
in the American Express
*then i knew **your soul**!*

BEADS

Beads of cheap glass   traded for human ass
shiney/ bright colors/ and ready to string
Beads from M.L. Levin, a British Jew, manufacturer of
slavers things (who progressed as his rich business grew!)
Beads used by traders in West Africa for   ivory/   for gold/palm oil/
   and us black slaves
faceted pieces of elongated glass (tons of it!)
used by the depraved
These beads called   jew-elry that robbed us blacks
of life's greatest treasure
These beads traded to dumb black chieftans
who sold us   for his beaded pleasure

IN GAO / OUTER GAO

GAO   in   and out   windows flies and mosquitos
Gao going and ungone   doors of straw   and   cloth
Gao   in   and   out   again   the canoe   is sewn   like a sock
Gao   cant get going   drivers of truck dreams
Gao   to go   Gao to   stay   there   is no get   away   in
Gao   where Russians pick   flowers   Tuareg tombstone   slabs of
      salt
get   going   into bits and pieces   like I   in Gao

TOP CREEP

Criminals Investigating Americans(C.I.A.)Faggots Bullying
                                             Indirectly(F.B.I.)

He spie / she   spy /   we cry / they shy / he cry / she sigh/we lie/
                                             they die!

LONG GONE LOVER BLUES

WHERE WAS YOUR LOVER   WHEN THE SAD SAD SUN
                                               WENT DOWN??

WHERE WAS YOUR LOVER WHEN THE BAD BAD MAN
                                               CAME AROUND?

THE SUN LEFT YOU IN THE DARK,and the bad man spit on

heart! So WHERE WAS YOUR LOVER THAT DAY??????????????

WHERE WAS YOUR LOVER WHO KNEW WHAT TO DO
                                               IN YOUR BED?

WHERE WAS YOUR LOVER WHO KNEW HOW TO PUMP LIFE
                                               IN THE DEAD?

YOUR BED WAS EMPTY AND COLD from making love with your body
and no soul   SO WHERE HAS YOUR LOVER DON' GONE?
WHERE WAS LOVER   WHY DID HE LEAVE YOU SO FAST?
WHERE WAS YOUR LOVER WHO HELP CHANGE
                                               YOUR UGLY PAST?
I HEARD HE IS DOWN SOUTH   WITH A SMILE ON HIS MOUTH AND
the sun shines bright on him all the day long . . . I heard he
is down south   with a smile on his mouth and the sun shines
bright on him   all the day long . . . .
                                     YES I HEARD HE'S
DOWN SOUTH   WITH A SMILE   ON HIS MOUTH
                                               AND THE SUN
SHINES BRIGHT ON HIM ALL THE DAY LONG!!!!!!!!!!!!!!!!

FAYFRIENDS

YOU CARED
YOU DECLARED
YOU DARED
YOU AIRED
YOU BARED
YOU NEVER SQUARED
SO I PROMISE AT
REVOLUTION DAY
YOU SHALL BE SPARED

THIS POEM IS

this poem is
> black as magic in Africa

this poem is
> read across counties, interstates plus international
>> lines

this poem is
> dangerous to the violent and a threat to evil's
>> overt actions

this poem is
> deceptive and sometimes severely silent before guilty
>> oat   meal   faces

this poem is
> inspiring third world's real scene, the fed-up
>> colored races

this poem is
> organizing the mass sons of soul with incendiary truths

this poem is
> promoting pride of Africa's future and great past

this poem is
> inciting us to self defense

this poem is
> not sitting on whitey's knee or an individual fence

this poem is
> the beacon of freedom now

this poem is
> the jazz shout

this poem is
> the switchblade knife cutting the faces of Washington

this poem is
> ready today . . . . . NOW . . . . this   hour!

this poem is
> the blackman (he who never cowers)

for he is this poem
> at this hour

together we are
> the poem   Forever   B L A C K   P O W E R!

Black Power!   Black Power!   Black Power!

GOTTA GIT . . .

White Cowboys carry guns to do violence
    "   Comic strips make laughs of violence
    "   Gangsters live and plan eternal violence
    "   Television and radio instruct violence
    "   Christians do blessed violence
    "   World's military and police act violence
    "   Politicians promise or advise violence
So in the name of self-defense
We black folks with some sense - Gotta git . . .

93

NO BLUES WITH EROS

What should we do
When we are alone together
Where no one can see
Who we are naked (or nude)
Why should we refuse
    to share / this truth / this love /
    at this moment
How could we deny Eros - thus lose
    our marvelous magic
      We must not give the blues

THORNY

the thorns have the points
those thorns the bush trees grow
they are wise and grey
sharper than needles tips
they can draw quick blood
hot or cold from
mechanical white
electric gauge sight
blow darted big city guerillas
those thorn bearers are killers

MY ACE OF SPADES

MALCOLM X spoke to me & sounded you
   Malcolm X said this to me, then told you that
   Malcolm X whispered in my ears but screamed on you
   Malcolm X praised me and thus condemned you
   Malcolm X smiled at me and sneered at you
   Malcolm X covered me and exposed you
   Malcolm X made me PROUD and you all got scared
   Malcolm X told me to hurry and you begin to worry
   Malcolm X sung to me but growled at you
   Malcolm X freed me and frightened you
   Malcolm X told it like it *damn shor* is!
He said I gotta fight to be really FREE
     Malcolm X told both of us
        the truth, now didn't he?

MAMMA DRUM

tribute to black african drums

big mamma drum with your voice sweet and heavy
like a choir of summer thunder
buttocks round curving your   rapid sounds
of sexual delights exciting lovers in a flash like lightning

big tall mamma drum skin tight vagina loose and open to receive
a masculine thrust from a hard branch of bare baobab
covered with long gone bird's chalky dung

Shapely mamma drum sagging breast pointing at the   earth
from which you grew up leaving only your feet to
caress it with throbbing rhythms
you confess it the earth is you
mamma drum!   mamma drum!   tom-tom   mamma drum
    mamma drum tom-tom!
mamma drum mamma drum   mamma drum mamma drum
    mamma drum mamma drum

P O W - W O W

Listen to me colored brothers
Hear me shout our song
we all are well aware
of how long we all been done wrong
We all know
white has to go
out of our lives
like long long time ago
  No more imperialism/paternalism/capitalism/ or forced communism
    for you!
Unity is our thing/to swing!!
Unity is what
we many colored
nations must do
to get our face
out of the white
butt And
start a life a new!THATS WHAT!!

CUSTOMS & CULTURE?

perhaps what beans & potatos
mean to me is what
cornflakes & yoghurt mean to you
maybe the machines tell your insides
something similar to what the
drums inspire in me
do you really believe cold weather is
invigorating as the sunshine
is fine everyday everyway for me all the time
if you really think your way is right and fine
then why do you pass laws against mine?

KA-CHOO!!

Africa   can play serious   tricks on   the misinformed
African weather can change real quick & to yr health do great harm
So when you to Africa go   take warm clothing & medicines more
for at night it can be quiet cold   thats time evil spirits in-filtrate
                                                    your body & soul
from Tangier,Agades,Sebha,Tit & Kissidougou   you'll worship evil
                                                          spirits
by shouting: Ka-choo! Ka--cho o! Ka-C H O O ! !

BUCKLE

to leroi jones

In the crazy quilt/ of many colors/ AFRICA!
frm the Tropic of Capricorn & Cancer   & the soft rope of visible
    Equator
the whole world is held   together   by the buckle found only in
    AFRICA!
    In distant grains of sand   lying like turtles on their backs
one can always find the food/sex / & Art of humanity   smiling like
    an advertisment for good health
Here/ in all the two eyed animals bellys/ lies the secret of
    skyscrapers collages with gonorrhea infested with cotton
    ball-bearings breath
If ever/ the hairy flying fish of Africa's rivers shits with a cough!
then   that rest of the world who is always 'dreaming of a white
    xmas'
when that buckle of the earth belt opens   the regimes/
    governments/parties &
policies all over this earth   will fall down faster than a Call-Girl's
underpants! I've seen MAUMAU in London/Paris & Manhattan
just as powerful or black powerful for what its worth
    Yet/   here
in Timbuctu   I found the secret of you & the world's girth

FACES

I want to see faces

of all races/winning faces/grinning faces/happy faces/faces that face East in prayer/faces covered & uncovered with hair/faces up lifted & proud/faces of joy of being in love/faces of yesterday,today,NOW & tomorrow faces/faces that erased war/faces that destroyed ignorance,disease, & hunger/faces that faced the tasks & won/freedom faces/freedom faces/faces of one nation and that nation is the human being congregation of faces/freedom faces/I want to see faces/I want to see faces/I want to see faces/I want to face me

SEVEN

There was seven
There were seven chairs
Here behind the long long table
There were seven empty chairs
These chairs were soon occupied
These seven men were well known authorities
These seven authorities sat behind the long long table
They   were the seven authorities on   black people
They   were   those seven   men who were often quoted concerning
                                        black people
These seven authorities talked of black people
These seven authorities advised officials about black people
These seven authorities manifested for black people
These seven authorities were well paid for their views about
                                        black people
These seven authorities   had written numerous   books about
                                        black people
There were seven sitting there in seven chairs talking about
                                        black people
The only thing wrong   about this 'magnificent' seven
was that
this seven   were not at all right   and too they were all W H I T E !

SISSY GAL

cornflakes   cut & make   chewing gums ache   during
drugstore   milkshakes   many   teenagers hearts break
with   their nine month   belly ache   that always explodes
or   sexplodes like an   Afro   American earthquake   mothers
that   work & moan & groan 'for heavens sakes' telling you to
stay   a-way   from   the   football
basketball   &   bowling   alley   fakes You . . . you know?
that   white   garden hoe?   that sharp black digging spade?
               and of course   that damn dangerous
straight pronged   farmer's rake!   Oh Well   in spite of your
                  teenage night   your brother's your pal
                  big belly and all My Sissy Gal!

LAST NIGHT IN NEWARK

Last night   in Newark   summer Newark
We black men three and sister soul in back
rode Volkswagen bus cutting our way through hot
humid Newark summer Newark   a city of vacant lust
Then out of nowhere   white they came
rude/ crude/ oatmeal pale & lame
following our bus   with their sneers & frowns
muttering their Italian accented cuss at us
We black three with sister soul in back
They pull up beside to provoke   in Newark summer Newark
but before they could say 'boy'
they were greeted with abarrage of black poetry
from LeRoi
          in Newark   summer Newark
we three/LeRoi/ a blood/ sister soul
                              & me
the wop cops had to flee
                    in Newark   summer Newark
it was the wrong bus for them to cuss
                         in Newark summer Newark

SOUTHERN LANDSCAPERS

to Jim Haynes/Paul Bowles/ & Charles Henri Ford (all friends)

The southern landscape don' changed Jim/
the strange fruit is booby-trapped watermelons/
the 'nice coloured man' is a killer guerilla/
& the only black folks that 'hang' around
are armed in the shadows of city hall
The southern landscape don' gone 'n' changed Paul/
the uncle Toms say Sir with Tommy guns/
the pickaninys don't beg for pennies
they take their share from behind a desk downtown
& Ol' black Mammy sits up front on Greyhound buses
 cleaning her nails with a switchblade
& its 'IN' to call a spade a spade!
The southern landscape has gone good wid change Charles/
the darkies aint 'gay' today/
they jess spy on the faggot F.B.I. &
cry/BLACK POWER! so loud,makes a white man cower/
 & they've gone 'n' taken the word 'nigger'
it is official in their hands way I figger
Yes Siree,the southern landscape don' changed a bit
You alls better stay over seas cause if you all aint changed
 you all sho' cant fit   thangs don' gone good wid change!!

THERE SHE IS

to Mrs.Zella Jones

There she is   sitting across from jazz giants and blues mammies
There she is astride a great elephant's head riding to   glory
  There she is wearing green slacks,pink high heels and no bra
  There she is strutting her stuff in the Easter commercial parade
There she   is   chasing sparrows from front porch window floor
There she is naked as a jaybird down south swimming with other
                    color women screaming joyfully in mid summer sun
There she is cleaning chitterlings with a frown but never putting'em
                                                                    down
There she is walking with a pregnant soul on the levee
  There she is floating up and down the Mississippi and Ohio river
There she is doing black back country dances and prances
There she is in front of wooden school house,wooden church,and
                                        with wooden pose for camera
There she is holding a water moccasin on a hickory stick
there she is decorating xmas trees the stars from her eyes shine
  there she is combing her first child's hair forward then to the side
there she is holding her son's hand crossing the dirty slum streets
there she is swimming without a blanket toward the North
  there she is sitting at the counter waiting for pennies from hell
there she is wearing burlap bags around her feet to fight the cold
there she is arming herself with an iron poker against the collector
there she is lying,crying and trying to keep her children from jails
there she is searching for leftovers,second hand-me-downs, and trash
there she is spending wisely on foodstuffs and fuel stuffs
  there she is shouting in storefront congregation
  there she is crying at a funeral for her man
  there she is doing a Sit-In,Wade-In,Ride-In and Shit-In
there she is with mustard,ketchup, salt & pepper placed in her hair
there she is de-segregating the home of the brave trying to be free
there she is praying Lord Have Mercy no more
there she is refusing to sing We Shall Overcome

there she is visiting Detroit,Chicago,New York,Los Angeles

                                         & to learn

there she is making Molotov cocktails and humming Burn Baby Burn

 there she is telling whitey to get out of her way

there she is my statue of Liberty my freedom symbol and no other

there she is black & beautiful brave & active   my mother!

MELLOW YELLOW

She's white
He's black
and she figures
that he digs her
She's wrong
He's right
For his Chinese chick
is just *out of sight*!

THE HAT

it sits there
it sits right over there
it sits there alone and proud
it sits overthere waiting for a head
it always gets a head
it was made for getting a head
it must be musical with its band
it is one of the best
it is always covering up
it is forever non square
it can not be worn on the ass
it can be understood by all
it has fought with the elements
it is my hat
it is my hat that you've hung
it is my hat that is guilty
it is my hat that runs away with the wind
it is my hat your broadbutt sits upon
it is my hat that is left on the rack
it is my hat from everywhere
it is my hat that is tip'ed
it is my hat that talks to my brain
it is my hat that is my crown
it is my hat   it is my hat   it is my hat   it is
                            my hatIT IS MY HAT!!
oh hell — I'm wearing my cap!

IN HOMAGE TO HEAVY LOADED TRANE, J.C.

J.C. in these
sentences of three
read by
Stokely C. Allen G. & me
London summer '67
J.C. it said:
sheets of sound
S   e   r   p
                    e
                        n
                          t
                            i
                              n e   screams   of happiness
hot molted masses of marvelous messages
and   HEAVY   anger
                        p
                          o
                            u
                              r
                                i
                                  n
                                    g
                    forth   from   fiery   throats
of your thick reeds
spurting rhythms
all over
all under
and all around
J.C.
Mr. Trane
J.C.
John Coltrane
with pain
we read
three short English lines

of your dying
and we strain
J.C.
black people & me
to keep
from crying

NADJA RENDEZVOUS

to André Breton

I first read his works in June 1942
I met him in June 1960
I last saw him in June 1966
I was going to see him again in 1967 June
but The Glass of Water in the Storm(1713)
of 4-2-rue Fontaine kept an almost forgotten
rendezvous with Nadja/in the Magnetic Fields/
she with her Convulsive Beauty/Legitimet Defense/
to protect herself from L'Air de l'Eau/   Au Lavoir
Noir/   Nadja sitting naked waiting with her
body spread out like the sky at midnight . . Yes a
L'Amour Fou/ in Arcane 17/a Claire de Terre/L'Humour noir/
images left as keys in the mail box
The revolver . . the white haired revolver is still loaded!

NITTY GRITTY

Hey moon faced female with your under wear on upside down!!
Why do you have some much kinky hair . . . between your fat legs?
I know what you thinking   I have been drinking! No you're wrong
I happy,loud and crude   When I open my mouth I just sound rude
Hey brownface gal and pale face bitch! I want to go to
bed with you!

I'm rough,and ready I wont sleep with you nor let you get any sleep
I am a city cowboy that rides women instead of horses and sheep
Call the police I dont give a damn they'll give us some rubbers!
Dial the phone backwards bitch and you'll get god!
take off your clothes baby . . I want to really see you!
I feel for you so now I am feeling good   Rape you with my eyes!
skin back a banana for me baby! Lets get hi!
I'll light a joint while you powder your hole with gold dust
Tomorrow I'm gonna marry your mother
Then you two will have me in the family
Each day and night I'll make everything all right
Did you hear what I said . . Now tell me what did I say?

BELIEVE YOU ME!

I am going back
I am black   but I'm going back
A young Russian poet I once read;
"a poet should be where the action is"
  thats what he said
I am going back
I'm going to   r e t u r n
to the land of   Burn,Baby,B u r n !
I am going back
I'm going back and play real dumb
  join hands with Whitey and sing
"We Shall Overcome"
Yeah I'm going back (not some day)
I'm going back to the police/dogs/firehoses/night sticks/day sticks/
  harassment/jail/ pushed & shoved/spat on/shot at/aggravated/hated/
  cheated & chased/fought & framed/fined,mis-judged guilty/kicked
  & refused/beat up/put down/thrown out & locked in/fenced off/
  choked off/castrated/segregated & separated/shuned & runned/
  unrewarded & discarded/cold & hungry/sickly & shut out/ thats
  what America is
all about!!Robbed,Raped, and Ruined/ as we non-violently faced the
white mobs with our songs
Leaped on,Lashed at,and Lynched / when we prayed to enter better
  housing and schools   Beaten,Brutalized, and Bombed/We U.S.
  niggers were the White world's number one fools!   You've got the
  money/ the bomb/ & guns/ the police/your laws/& army its all
  your own fun
But I'm not afraid   and I'm too damn tired to run
  I am going back
with a mission up my sleeve
Lets just call it:*jazz poetry*
JAZZ   IS   NON- VIOLENT
Yeah thats what I want White America to believe   I'm going back!

115

MANNIKIN BOY OF BRUSSELS

                  S H E
              AND
          ME
              WENT TO
                  BELGIUM
                      TO SEE
                          A STATUE
                              PEE
                                  AND
                                      IT DID
                                          PISS
SO   SHE   AND   ME STOOD THERE AND   WE
                                      K I S S E D

GRI-GRIS

I got my eyes,ears,mouth,nose and toes telling my teeth what to do
   when why,how, & to whom what for
I carried my switchblade from Harlem tribe through the dangerous
   dangers of Deutschland & Britain fog thick with uncouth thugs
   of traditional burlap & barbedwire parents
I supported my gri-gris spirits in deep xmas morn snow south of Oslo
   where rolled peanuts butterballed across Place Concorde caving in
   a Russian Nazi's pad twice in Malaga there they say tomorrow
   nuns will snore
I displayed my gri-gri on the bare bellys of Bulgarian beauties lying
   spread eagle (but hiding their slits) on burning beaches of Jugo
   not too distant from Split where my cravat's knot came from
   California redwood
I infested ten tons of new born hyenas with four-eyed shirts thus
   admitting once & for all times the existence of ball-bearings-
   banana peel marriages yet shoelaces crusted with stars,flies,
   funnels,molasses,3-D throwaway glasses incased in silk pages of
   books on Slanted Cum from North Vietnam: will still overcome
   as houndog hully gully says SUM-Die!
I carry at all times a radio up my asshole to inform Washington,
   Peking,Paris,Moscow,Madrid,Little Rock & Hammerfest of all
   open vaginas windows tormented aardvarks embryos and
   celestial coiffures on desert donkeys
I can not forget 1828 was only one hundred years before I was
   born that René Caillie went to Timbuctu (later a fennec frighten
   him in tangier) there he bought Mungo Park's tape recorder for
   six old Mali Empire cowrie francs by standing the postman
   upside down behind a Tokyo toilet removing dentist drills
I sat this hot xmas morn covered with Koranic incantations
   in leather bags watching a bat & owl dance sideways in memory
   of Malcolm X who signed my photo in Paris under boogie
   woogie queens gaze (kif smoke serves as under arm deodorant!)
I tote gri-gri tonight in Yankee Doodle den being well protected
   from new camels,stranded Cadillacs,copper plated corn flakes &

antique lace gloves with builtin limp wrist with glowing face
watch that alarms gloves that love along the ocean front where
fish walk back & forth carrying flags made of can openers and
the latest ladies underwear centers
I conjured up & down seven giraffes backs in Gao giving them a free
trip to Harlem via Watts Happenings on A-Train but bib overalls
ran smack past our subway stop driving with his false finger in
his wooden nose now bidons of prophylactic wax wait in the
tallest building in Ft Lamy(my socks were green!)
I wore gri-gri instead of fashionable clothing & hairbrushes to
mystical Montana mother's beds those filthy pieces of suggestive
& misused muebles disowned & disrobed basket weaver spat
fireballs & snowdoughnuts(my foot is right now!)
I can not speak gri-gri with some fork that my truck driver rakes
Italian Chinese imported spaghetti crumbs around dirty dog liver
churches crowded Crowsday with mad musicians pangolins who
ate roaring under table hairs you can no longer enlighten Danish
cheese sleepers or Nairobi airport hustlers A giant Senoufo mask
made love to the Empire state building & refused red ant a
photograph inspite police badge threats covered with
congressional homosexual events from sweden Finns with
Congolese nun virgins sang sideways yet cups with sexy saucers
under stayed high on the way up the thigh of Jutland where
several more trucks tip-toed in ditches getting dirty being
shy-like   like vinegar
Certainly one of my grandest gri-gris glowed gladily each time we
crossed Manhattan,Milano,Malmo and Mopti manhole covers
secretly designed by Franz Kline just before the Cedar tavern
moved to supermarket sheet wearers turf (my scrotum is as
wrinkled as a prune's uncle's flashlight beam)
It was gri-gri that caused the death of your destructive devilmen of
tall Tuetonic temple torn ideologies by cyclone barefeet we
swore in Texas to do baked eggs & pillow duty to stop God &
Our Country before they would be alone & being salesmen with
no clients for motor vests & concrete grey roaches with dayglo
shoelaces they would die near a cemetery cheaply(Can you have
dinner over for lunch tomorrow & still invite supper's tongue?)

A headline from Bobo land read in black tongues: "No More Ostrich
Eggs Can Be Brought to Bougival" those Romans that read daily
under bridges read on until words themselves ceased to be names
of images brassieres,bannisters,borrowed trench coats with-torn
epaulettes or cloth caps of Irish oars men off the coast of
Abidjan where horned vipers dressed as blackberrys with triangle
shaped balls throw well known curse words at sex-starved
Peacorniks with mixed razor blades,broken branches of Turkish
trees that constantly remind one of malnutrition of cunt we will
have to be discontented with saturday night singing in night air
of Akron & Accra but Nude Collages & Naked Poems should be
marvelously shoved out between Munich's shapely checkered
thighs

Onto Gorée island they say that godamned slave marketeer threw
my ancestor gri-gri away into a sharks pit,placed my griot grand
grand great daddy on sugar cane peanut and awful looking water
diet for twenty seven days & twenty nine nights when ever frogs
underpants find their favorite guitar strings broken they seldom
ever sold human beings to sun hating animals for cases of Johnny
walker,Cutty Sark,Black&White Play Boy copies or glues

It was gri-gri held in a soft kind hand of the kinky head agent who
caused revolutions against pomades,caviar and   yellow fever
favorites baseballing from chick to tit bearing factory flying
water statues plain glass over blind mountain stops during
Ramadan with rhythm sleeping against Baobab trees in
sparkplug forest weeping spiders tears covering every tone in
balafon   breast plate glaring umbrellas ribs with piement
protection never to growl a grown up statement like a peeing
Pole that reads Twi twice

It was the gri-gri collected for André Breton's tomb clock that
object that functions symbolical as fetish of Paris finally fetish
de France really the fetish du Monde causing governments to
issue defense de fetish they not hip enough to know that Breton
knew the only thing inevitable is change thus avoiding silly
stomach banners,LSD buttons that giggle: WOW! or crude war
slogans about chains found in Rotterdam's flea market make
damp days glow blue by summers sunset in the Sahara

It was gri-gri from the cliff dweller that Dogon dancer of tall
    masques who made Mississippi Lester Young believe in
    kilometers of python skin designs drying his tongue too tight
    getting bitter between stiff reeds of Nubia or Helsinki via
    Carbondale   during morning erections without thoughts of
    rubber vaginas bouncing more pounds than the once every
    marvelous minute in it (the carload of shit arrived on stage late)
It was gri-gri that caused horns of cows to blow up in Chad

    afterwards the plane bearing Svensk cat of the U.N. was slapped
    by lightning that walks from the skies Lumumba phamtoms
    smoked pot in celebration around paranoiac Paris places where
    Brazzaville bandits who crooked F.D.R. wheel chair wheels
    causing the empty chair to cave thousands of bats with
    flutterby masks on cadmium lips oxen orange buttocks
    typewriter ribbon red rumps rolled forward for future racial
    shoving finally an Austrian dons a turtle neck causing an
    American assassin to cough chuckles as he admits on television
    before his wife smiles of admiration that he and he alone was the
    official bullet that married birds gri-gri on toast in Pennsylvania
    bus station late October 1946 overcoat belt
Gri-gri seven lucky shells out of torn pocket tattered from
    Timbuctoo's table edge those cowries jacked off an ancient get
    up used even today by modern mad hipster for international
    putdown an Australian heavy hitchiking heifer bent over in
    Gibraltar night cave high up above band aids and thin ham
    sandwiches
Gri-gri is billed as a Western titled as usual "A Stick Up at Skin Back
    Bend" galloping down nigger streets naked in the winter at dawn
    trigger pulled over like a Norwegian sweater at ski-time when
    soft sand of Bidon Cinq sank Volkswagen bus boys sunk down
    behind the police car to shoot it out with a finger
Gri-gri of the Tropic of Cancer in desolate desert of Reg & Erg
    blackening blue men & women   Gri-gri on my canoe that
    pirogues down the Nigeriver paddle by long stick that gooses
    your sky nodding its approval since nobody is in an American
    hospital now   Gri-gri in bowels of Bamako & Boston
    backwards Gri-gri found on the streets of Ouagadougou near

the Moro-Naba's palace Gri-gri laying under a market mama's
dress proving that rhinoceroses can sell movie pictures   gri-gri
of Sahara saheb dried bones deserted goat horns trumpeting
stories to be read naked in public   gri-gri wrapped in hair and
horse manure carried in an ambassador's briefcase   gri-gri
going across the airport runway chasing raindrops spoonful at
a time gri-gri sticking out like an obscene Floridia warning young
girls to keep their legs open & minds closed   gri-gris who dont
love cars trucks doorknobs guns toothpicks & brushes   gri-gris
that wonder who dies at once when shadows of astronauts burn
brighter   gri-gri the good   gri-gri the bad   gri-gri up her
ass   gri-gri down his throat   gri-gri   now & forever in dry toilets
gri-gri under the baldness of a seal's head gri-gri supporting rims
of glasses made of bamboo   gri-gri the graceful gri-gri the clumsy
tart   gri-gri between the teeth of sharpness of surrealism
gri-gri the long erected prick of jazz   gri-gri that can gri-gri that
could   gri-gri that has   gri-gri that will grow another finger
of gri-gri to nurse the walking breast of mother   gri-gri is the
black power that continues man's greatest climax just after
humping along a dusty trail looking for the wrinkled page of
prose found now and then poets whores worldly called: a muse!

J.F.K.* B L U E S

Because of him there is a fire burning in an Alaskan igloo tonight
Because of him there is a freedom bus smashing the wall of East
Berlin
Because of him there will always be a guilty expression on faces
from Dallas

So if he is dead . . . . Oh No, oh no oh no!

Because of him there is a T.V. antenna on Uncle Tom's splitlevel
cabin
Because of him the world waits for Godot and pennies from heaven
Because of him Federal stars fell on Alabama to allow Martin Luther
King to ride a bus up front

So if he is dead . . . . Oh No oh no oh no!

Because of him U.S. passports are now the color of Caroline's
innocent eyes
Because of him rhinoceroses are riding jetplanes to Japan and
Holland
Because of him American spades dug deeper into their fight (day &
night) against Southern segregation & Northern discrimination

So if he is dead . . . . Oh No oh no oh no!

Because of him tears and laughter stream down between the breast
of a glove
Because of him the entire American nation swings back and forward
in a rocking chair
Because of him mighty powerful planes with megatonbombs are
singing peace is our profession

So if he is dead . . . . Oh No oh no oh no!

*Just, For, Kicks

Because of him mad men, mad dogs and high pressure fire hoses
    'had' to go down by the riverside
Because of him young Europe looked toward the U.S. for leadership
Because of him millions of Americans read faster and poets get alittle
    more respect

    So if he is dead . . . . Oh No oh no oh no!

Because of him a nuclear testban 'almost' banned that damn bomb
Because of him Red China called Red Russia an un-Marxist mother
    fucker!
Because of him many men parted their hair but kept their wives a
    little longer

    So if he is dead . . . . Oh No oh no oh no!

Because of him Cuban cigars and Cuban sugar are now Cuban cigars
    and Cuban sugar
Because of him culture became the thing in the U.S.A. and didnt
    Pop Art start!
Because of him for the first time in U.S. history jazz was played in
    the White House
Because of him new frontiers were started with that All-American
    'vigah'
Because of him Africa and Asia took their well timed GIANT steps
Because of him this generation was led by the youth
Because of him all the world's politicians had to tell somebody the
    truth
Because of him there is a growing passion for democracy and peace
    has become the ambition of practically all of mankind

So if he is really dead . . . . . then I ask you to bow your head and cry
On No   On No   OH NO!

TRUE BLUES FOR DUES PAYER

As I blew   the second chorus   of Old Man River
(on an old gold trumpet loaded with blackass jazz)
a shy   world traveling   white Englishman   pushed a
French-Moroccan
newspaper   under my   Afroamerican   brown eyes
there it said   that you were dead   killed by   a group
of black assassins   in black Harlem   in the black of night
As I read   the second page   of blues giving   news
(with wet eyes and trembling cold hands)
I stood   facing East   under quiet & bright   African sky
I didnt cry   but inside   said goodbye   to you whom
I confess

I loved   Malcolm X

THE BIG BLACK THREE

for Tony and Oba

the big black three
that includes me
wake up in   hot sweaty   ghetto room
the night's sleep we had   to escape slumgutter was glad
now into crowded sidewalk morning we stroll
fifty cents between   three grown men
thus three slices of watermelon we ate
breakfasting and digging chicks
especially natural hair-do's and Afro clothes:straight!
the big black three
that includes me
walk up the hot sunny ghetto streets
talking'n' laffing real loud
at the police heliocopter   spying in 'n' out ghetto clouds
'those motherfucking fuzz show wont leave us be' said he.
the big black three
that includes me
looking for work for money is our thing
the 'want-ads' dont want us   janitor jobs in Jersey are   too far out
   and if so   we aint got   enough money three fares on a bus
so the big black three
that includes me
loaf 'n' stroll up 'n' down ghetto gutters wide
so since whitey's got money like corn on the cob
our survival depends upon what we can take from him and rob
that is our task   the ghetto three   the black one   that
    includes me!

WHITE WOMAN

your face is pale   your love is hollow   but you are

real   when you give the dollar!

LITTLE BROWN BITCH BLUES (OR; I'VE GOT THE
SUN IN MY SOUL)

I want a little brown girl   I want to love her a lot
I want to give a black gal   everything I've got
I'm feeling good   I've got the sun in my soul

I want a big black woman   I want to jazz her day'n'night
I want a short brown lady with whom I'll never fuss'n'fight
I'm feeling groovy
I've got the sun in my soul

I want a blue black chick   that makes other women look sad
Maybe a pale blonde bitch   to make Uncle Sam mad
I'm feeling great
I've got the sun in my soul

You can have a yellow woman
You can have   a mellow tan gal
You can have a hincty pink pin-up   that puts out to everybody
even to your best pal
So I'll take a small brown babe   and place her in my bag
I'll give   her food/ sex/ and Art   then she'll never nag
Man, I'm feeling boss, I've got the sun in my soul
Yes,doing swell, I've got the sun in my soul

THE SUN MY SON
dedicated to the first woman I ever slept with, my   mother

if only the sun would shine to night

       the   m o o n   would   seem twice brighter

if only the sun would shine   tonight

       white boy you'd seem w h i t e r

purple cows
pulling golden plows
through a marshy   toilet

woolen brassieres
wornout by years
pink   light red   and   scarlet

if only the sun would shine tonight

       the moon   could   sleep   till morning

if   only   the sun   would shine   to night

       there would   never be no d a w n i n g

THE NICE COLORED MAN

Nice Nigger Educated Nigger Never Nigger Southern Nigger
Clever Nigger Northern Nigger Nasty Nigger Unforgivable Nigger
Unforgettable Nigger Unspeakable Nigger Rude & Uncouth Nigger
Mean & Vicious Nigger Smart Black Nigger Smart Black Nigger
Smart Black Nigger Smart Black Nigger Smart Black Nigger Smart
Black Nigger   Smart Black Nigger   Smart Black Nigger Knife
Carrying Nigger Gun Toting Nigger Military Nigger Clock Watching
Nigger Food Poisoning Nigger Disgusting Nigger Black Ass Nigger
Black Ass Nigger Black Ass Nigger Black Ass Nigger Half White
Nigger Big Stupid Nigger Big Dick Nigger Jive Ass Nigger Wrong
Nigger Naughty Nigger Uppity Nigger Middleclass Nigger
Government Nigger Sneaky Nigger Houndog Nigger Grease Head
Nigger Nappy Head Nigger Cut Throat Nigger Dangerous Nigger
Sharp Nigger Rich Nigger Poor Nigger Begging Nigger Hustling
Nigger Whoring Nigger Pimping Nigger No Good Nigger Dirty
Nigger Unhappy Nigger Explosive Nigger Godamn Nigger
Godamnigger Godamnigger Godamnigger Godamnigger
Godamnigger Godamn Nigger Godamnigger Godamnigger
Godamnigger Godamnigger Godamnigger

                                        Neat Nigger Progressive
Nigger Nextdoor Nigger Classmate Nigger Roomate Nigger Laymate
Nigger Weekend Date Nigger Dancing Nigger Smiling Nigger Ageless
Nigger Old Tired Nigger Silly Nigger Hippy Nigger White Folks
Nigger Integrated Nigger Non-Violent Nigger Demonstrating Nigger
Cooperative Nigger Peaceful Nigger American Nigger
Uneducated Nigger Under Rated Nigger Bad Nigger Sad Nigger
Slum Nigger Jailhouse Nigger Stealing Nigger Robbing Nigger
Raping Nigger
                    Lonely Nigger Blues Singing Nigger Dues
Paying Nigger Unemployed Nigger Unwanted Nigger
Impossible Nigger Cunning Nigger Running Nigger Cruel Nigger
Well Known Nigger Individual Nigger Purple Nigger Beige
Nigger Bronze Nigger Brown Nigger Red Nigger Bed Nigger
Yellow Nigger Tan Nigger Mulatto Nigger Creole Nigger
Inevitable Nigger Mixed Up Nigger Slave Nigger Unfree Nigger
Savage Nigger Jazz Nigger Musical Nigger Godamnigger

Godamnigger Godamnigger Godamnigger Godamnigger
Godamnigger Jesus Loves Us Nigger Preaching Nigger We Shall
Overcome Nigger Someday Nigger Militant Nigger Real Nigger
Brave Nigger Real Nigger Violent Nigger Real Nigger Intelligent
Nigger Real Nigger Active Nigger Real Nigger Wise Nigger Real
Nigger Deceitful Nigger Real Nigger Courageous Nigger Real
Nigger Cool Nigger Real Nigger Hip Nigger Real Nigger Hot
Nigger Real Nigger Funky Nigger Real Nigger (I Cant Figger
This Nigger He's Too Much This Nigger! He's All Over Us This
Nigger I Dont Trust This Nigger He's Far Too Much He's
Everywhere . . . . . This Nigger!)

Eeny Meeny Minee Mo
Catch Whitey By His Throat
If He Says—Nigger   C U T   I T ! !

Printed in the USA
CPSIA information can be obtained
at www.ICGtesting.com
LVHW091135150724
785511LV00001B/158